Landscapes of
SOUTHERN
TENERIFE
AND
LA GOMERA

a countryside guide
Second edition

Noel Rochford

SUNFLOWER
BOOKS

Dedicated to Simon, Maria and Matthew

Second edition
Copyright © 1995
Sunflower Books
12 Kendrick Mews
London SW7 3HG, UK

First edition 1988

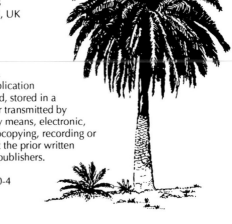

ISBN 1-85691-050-4

Important note to the reader

We have tried to ensure that the descriptions and maps in this book are error-free at press date. The book will be updated, where necessary, whenever future printings permit. It will be very helpful for us to receive your comments (sent in care of the publishers, please) for the updating of future printings.

We also rely on those who use this book — especially walkers — to take along a good supply of common sense when they explore. Conditions change fairly rapidly in the Canaries, and ***storm damage or bulldozing may make a route unsafe at any time***. If the route is not as we outline it here, and your way ahead is not secure, return to the point of departure. ***Never attempt to complete a tour or walk under hazardous conditions!*** Please read carefully the notes on pages 45 to 49, 121 and 128, as well as the introductory comments at the beginning of each tour and walk (regarding road conditions, equipment, grade, distances and time, etc). Explore ***safely***, while at the same time respecting the beauty of the countryside.

Cover: La Fortaleza, La Gomera, from the north (photograph: Andreas Stieglitz)
Title page: house on La Gomera
Photographs by the author, except for those on pages 24-25 (John Underwood), 22, 52-53, 108 (Andreas Stieglitz)
Maps by John Theasby and Pat Underwood
Drawings by Sharon Rochford
A CIP catalogue record for this book is available from the British Library.
Printed and bound in the UK by Brightsea Press, Exeter
6 5 4 3 2 1

Contents

4 Landscapes of Southern Tenerife and La Gomera

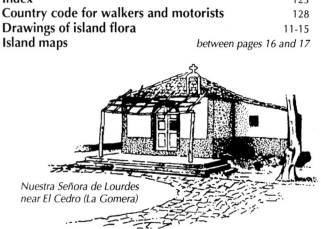

Nuestra Señora de Lourdes
near El Cedro (La Gomera)

❋ Preface

Few places in the world can offer the kaleidoscope of natural beauty found in the Canary Islands. What one island lacks, another has in plenty. Each island has a personality of its own.

The south of Tenerife, where most readers who use this guide will be staying, is associated with bodies and beaches. Few visitors explore beyond the compulsory coach tour to El Teide. They may return home thinking of Tenerife's landscape as barren, however magnificent. They have missed the laurel forests of the Anaga and the soft green valleys of the Teno Peninsula. The car tours described in this book put the entire island within your reach. *Do* get out and explore — you'll be surprised! You may even be enticed to get to know the entire island in depth. If so, the walks and picnics in the companion volume, *Landscapes of Tenerife,* will put the Teno and Anaga peninsulas, La Orotava and Las Cañadas at your fingertips.

As for walking in the south, hardly anyone thinks of it: the bleached façade of the interior looks rather unappealing. Besides, some think, it's always too hot and sunny. But during the winter months some days will be cool and cloudy, and they're ideal for walking. The five walks in the south of the island described here lead to exhilarating, unfrequented beauty spots. You'll venture upon canyon-sized ravines, gorges overflowing with vegetation, waterfalls and trickling streams — all well concealed in this 'bleak' landscape. These walks have been chosen for their easy access from the south.

When you've explored a bit on Tenerife, get to know nearby La Gomera. Unfamiliar to many by name, but tantalizingly close, this little dome-shaped island sits some 20 miles southwest of Los Cristianos — just an hour and a half away by ferry, or only 35 minutes by hydrofoil. The schedules allow you enough time to get there for a good day's car touring or walking. These daily sailings are La Gomera's only link with the outside world. The lack of an airport (see touring map for proposed site) has so far saved the island from the blight of mass tourism that has overtaken southern Tenerife.

La Gomera cannot offer you luxury hotels or discos

— not even air-conditioned coach tours. It's a more modest island, a place where one goes to appreciate the simple things in life, like peace and quiet, space to breathe and splendid rural scenery. In all three of these it excels, and, on top of this, the island remains beautifully unspoilt.

La Gomera is a walkers' paradise. But if you're not a walker, explore the island by car. Break up your tours with picnics or leg-stretching breaks along the paths to the picnic spots suggested on pages 11-15. Many of these picnic settings lie along the route of a long walk, so you can get the 'feel' of the landscape without hiking for miles. Perhaps, unawares, you will find yourself drawn deeper and deeper into the countryside.

Getting to know an island is getting to know the people, so before you set off, learn a few words of Spanish. The 'Gomeros' are a reserved people, up until the present unaffected by tourism. They have their work cut out for them in the fields. However, if you do speak some Spanish, you will find them responsive and helpful. (It's not likely that you'll have time to master the other 'language' spoken on La Gomera — the *silbo,* a centuries-old 'whistling language' developed by the Guanches to communicate across the enormous ravines that slice through the island...)

Whether you are exploring Tenerife or La Gomera, this book will help you to *find* something different, *taste* something different, and to *meet* someone different — the essence, I hope, of a memorable visit.

Acknowledgements

Special thanks to the following people for their invaluable help:
Angel Fernandez of ICONA, La Gomera, for information and maps;
Departments of Public Works, La Gomera and Tenerife, for maps;
Patronato de Turismo, Tenerife, for maps;
My sister, Sharon, for her lovely drawings;
John Theasby, for his maps;
My publisher, Pat Underwood, for her encouragement;
My parents and friends, always there to welcome me home from my travels.

Useful books

Bramwell, D, and Bramwell, Z *Wild flowers of the Canary Islands,* London, Stanley Thornes Ltd, 1984
Moeller, H *The flora of the Canary Islands,* Puerto de la Cruz, Fred Kolbe (latest edition available on the island)
Also available: Rochford, Noel *Landscapes of Tenerife (Teno • Orotava • Anaga • Cañadas), Landscapes of Gran Canaria, Landscapes of Lanzarote, Landscapes of Fuerteventura, Landscapes of La Palma and El Hierro.* All are published by Sunflower Books.

Getting about

Tenerife

With rental rales being so reasonable, the best way to get around the island is by **hiring a car** (or motorbike). **Coach tours** are also a popular way of seeing Tenerife. While **taxis** are usually for those with less time and more money, sharing can make them worthwhile.

If you're not pushed for time, the **local buses** are fun and inexpensive (enquire about 'TITSA BONO' faresavers). The plan on the following pages shows you where to board buses in Playa de las Américas and Los Cristianos. While Tenerife's bus network is very extensive, bear in mind that scheduling will not always permit you to take *long* walks, if you're going quite a distance from your base in the south. For instance, for Walks 2 and 3 you will have to arrange alternative transport.

La Gomera

The cost of **car hire** on this island is high compared with Tenerife but, especially if you're only visiting for a day or two, it is certainly the most efficient way of getting about. **Taxis** are of course available for hire (agree on the price before setting out), but there is also a **communal taxi** system — an excellent way of getting around. It's considerably cheaper than hiring a private taxi, but may cost you a little time, as you wait for a few more passengers: the more passengers, the cheaper the fare. Note that communal taxis only run between the main villages, and the fare is generally a fixed rate.

Local buses run in conjunction with ferry arrivals/ departures. Morning buses come from all around the island to bring passengers for the 08.00 departure; at midday they depart again with arrivals from Tenerife. By mid-afternoon they return to the capital in time to catch the 18.00 ferry departure. You'll find this (infrequent) service adequate for short walks and picnics. *Always double-check departure times and arrive early!* A plan of San Sebastián is on pages 8-9.

One of the statues of Guanche chieftains at La Candelaria on Tenerife (Car tours 3 and 4)

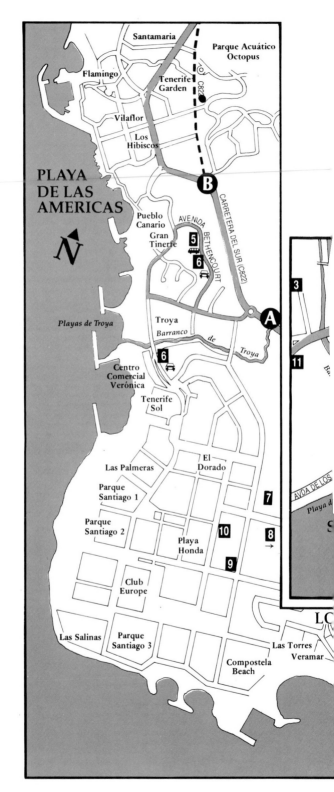

SAN SEBASTIAN

1 Casa de Colón; Post office;
   to Garajonay and Hermigua
2 Museum (Torre del Conde)
3 Hospital
4 Tourist office; Taxi rank
5 Town hall
6 Plaza de las Américas
7 Ferry/hydrofoil; Bus terminus
8 Parador Nacional
9 Nuestra Señora de la Asunción
10 Market
11 to Santiago, Valle Gran Rey
12 Main bus stop

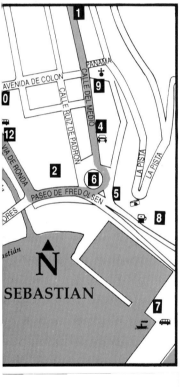

LOS CRISTIANOS/ PLAYA DE LAS AMÉRICAS

1 Ferry/hydrofoil
2 Post office
3 Bus stop (Los
   Cristianos)
4 Taxi rank (Los
   Cristianos)
5 Bus stop (Playa
   de las Américas)
6 Taxis (Playa
   de las Américas)
7 Football ground
8 Clinic
9 Public telephones
10 Police station

CONSULATES
Playa de las Américas
German (Avenida Anaga)
   Tel 28 48 12
Austrian (Calle San Fran-
   cisco) Tel 24 11 93
British (Calle Suarez
   Guerra) Tel 24 20 00
Danish (Avenida Anaga)
   Tel 27 57 57
French (Calle Méndez
   Núñez) Tel 27 53 27
Irish (Avenida Reyes
   Católicos) Tel 21 19 97
Norwegian (Calle Doctor
   Zerolo) Tel 28 72 50
Swedish (Avenida Anaga)
   Tel 27 33 16
Dutch (Calle La Marina)
   Tel 24 35 75

TELEPHONE NUMBERS
Airport 77 00 54
Ambulance 78 07 59
Fire station 22 00 80
First aid 70 09 97
Hospital 64 13 00
Medical centre 79 10 00
Police 78 02 26
   (Playa de las Américas)
Police 76 01 00
   (Los Cristianos)
Red Cross 78 07 59
Taxis 79 03 52
Taxis (Arona) 79 02 27
Taxis (Adeje) 79 14 07

Picnicking

Picnickers are extremely well catered for on both Tenerife and La Gomera. ICONA (Spain's national nature conservation agency) has set up several well-equipped 'recreation areas' around the islands. At these *zonas recreativas* (which tend to be crowded on weekends and holidays), you'll find tables, benches and drinking fountains. Many are also equipped with barbecues, WCs and play areas for children. On Tenerife these ICONA sites are to be found all over the island; on La Gomera they are dotted around the Garajonay National Park. All have been splendidly set up in total accord with their surroundings. All **roadside** picnic areas **with tables** (and sometimes other facilities) on both islands are indicated in the touring notes and on the touring maps by the symbol ⊼. The facilities available are also listed in the picnic or car touring notes.

This book also includes many other suggestions — for picnics 'off the beaten track', along the path of a walk. Four are included for Tenerife (there are some 35 others in the companion volume, *Landscapes of Tenerife*) and 11 for La Gomera. All the information you need to get to the suggested picnic spots is given on the following pages, where *picnic numbers correspond to walk numbers,* so that you can quickly find the general location on the island by referring to the appropriate pull-out touring map (where the walks are outlined in white). Most of these picnics are very easy to reach, and I outline transport details (🚌: which bus to take; 🚗: where to park), how long it will take you to walk to the picnic spot, and views or setting. Beneath the picnic title, you will also find a map reference: the location of the picnic spot is shown on this large-scale *walking* map by the symbol *P*. Some of the picnic settings are also illustrated; if so, a photograph reference follows the map reference.

Please glance over the comments before you start off on your picnic: if some walking is involved, remember to wear sensible shoes and to **take a sunhat** (○ indicates a picnic in *full sun*). It's a good idea to take along a plastic groundsheet as well, in case the ground is damp or prickly.

If you're travelling to your picnic by bus, be sure to verify bus departure times in advance. Although there are timetables at the back of the book (see page 114), they *do* change from time to time, without prior warning. **If you are travelling to your picnic by car**, be extra vigilant off the main roads: children and animals are often in the streets and may not be used to traffic. Without damaging plants, do park *well off* the road!

All picnickers should read the country code on page 128 and go quietly in the countryside. *Buen provecho!*

TENERIFE

1 BARRANCO DEL INFIERNO ○

Map page 51, photographs pages 50, 51
🚗 by car or taxi: 25-30min on foot. Park at the top end of Adeje, near the footpath to the *barranco*. Near Car tours 1 and 2
🚌 by bus: 1h30min on foot. Bus to Adeje (Timetables 7, 10).
Follow Walk 1 (page 50) as far as you like. Shade from the barranco walls only.

Red-flowering tabaiba (Euphorbia atropurpurea)

2 ARASA ○

Map page 55, nearby scene on pages 52-53
🚗 by car or taxi: up to 5min on foot. Park on the track to Arasa, an abandoned hamlet between Masca and Santiago del Teide. This is the *only* gravel track branching off west between Santiago and Masca. There's a viewpoint here. Leave your car where the track forks. Car tour 1
You can picnic at the outlook over the Masca Valley (a few minutes up the right-hand fork in the track; no shade) or else fork left, cross the (dry) stream and picnic above the wall, by a grassy area (no shade).

Verode (Senecio kleinia)

3 BARRANCO DE MASCA ○

Map page 55
🚗 by car or taxi: up to 1h on foot. Park above Masca village. Car tour 1
Follow Walk 3 (page 55), to picnic just before the bridge. Shade from rocks only.

5 PIEDRAS AMARILLAS ○

Map page 65, photograph pages 24-25
🚗 by car or taxi: 15-20min on foot. Park at the Parador de las Cañadas. Car tours 1, 2
🚌 by bus: 15-20min on foot. Bus to the Parador de las Cañadas (Timetable 4).
Follow Walk 5 (page 62), to the 'Yellow Stones' (no shade).

Lavandula pinnata

Senecio

Tenerife's *zonas recreativas*

(See touring map of Tenerife for ⊼-symbol. All have shade, tables, benches, water; settings described in the appropriate car tours.)

LA CALDERA (Car tour 1)
Barbecues, play area, toilets, bar/restaurant

LAS CAÑADAS ROAD (Car tour 1)
Six sites between Aguamansa and El Portillo

PICO DE LAS FLORES (Car tour 2)
Tables and benches; west of La Esperanza

Codéso (Adenocarpus foliolosus)

CHANAJIGA (near Car tour 1)
South of Los Realejos; barbecues; pine wood setting with wooden bridges, etc; toilets

EL LAGAR (near Car tour 1)
Just above La Guancha; barbecues, toilets

LAS ARENAS NEGRAS (near Car tour 1)
South of Icod de los Vinos; rough track; unusual black sand area; barbecues, toilets

LAS LAJAS (Car tour 1)

CHIO (Car tour 2)

ANAGA FORESTRY PARK (Car tour 4)
Barbecues, toilets

Margarita (Argyranthemum)

Tenerife: Short walk suggestions
Walk 1
Walk 2 (access by 🚌 only)
Walk 3, Short walk or Alternative walk 3-2 (access by 🚌 only)
Walk 4, Short walk
Walk 5, follow the main walk for 1h only

LA GOMERA

6a LOS ROQUES

Map page 68

Valo (Plocama pendula)

🚌 by car or taxi: 30min on foot. Park off the side of the San Sebastián/Valle Gran Rey road, near Roque de Agando. There is a sign for the Garajonay National Park here. Car tours 5, 6
Follow the footpath behind the sign; it heads down the crest of the ridge into the valley below. Some 25-30 minutes down, you reach an abandoned forestry house, from where there is a splendid view up to Los Roques. (Los Roques are shown on page 31). Shade. It's a stiff hour's climb back up!

6b MIRADOR DEGOLLADA DE PERAZA

Map page 68

Taginaste (Echium decaisnei)

🚌 by car or taxi: up to 5min on foot. Park at the (signposted) *mirador* (at the junction of the Santiago/San Sebastián roads). Car tour 5

🚐 By bus: up to 5min on foot. Bus to the Degollada de Peraza (Timetable 21).
Picnic anywhere down the path that leaves from the right of the mirador. You'll have a panorama over the Barranco de las Lajas and its reservoirs (these reservoirs are shown on page 68), as well as an outlook to Tenerife. Limited shade.

Cistus

8 CASAS DE PASTRANA

Map page 76

🚍 by car or taxi: 15-20min on foot. Follow the road just east of the Barranco de Santiago. This road is *not* signposted, but there is a public telephone just inside the turn-off. At the end of the road, fork right on a gravel track and park. Near Car tour 5
From here follow Walk 8 (page 75) from just after the 1h20min-point, to climb a rocky path to a higher track in Pastrana. Bear left and continue as far as the streambed crossing/gofio mill. A lovely spot, deep in a valley. Shade.

Sonchus ortunoi

9a ALAJERO ○

Map pages 80-81

🚍 by car or taxi: about 10min on foot. Park in the church square at Alajeró. Car tour 5
Follow the beginning of Walk 9 (page 79), to reach the quiet countryside vista over the elevated plains of the south. Picnic anywhere along the track, before the descent into the barranco. No shade in the immediate vicinity.

Palo sangre
(Sonchus tectifolius)

9b MIRADOR DEL IGUALERO

Map page 80

🚍 by car or taxi: up to 5min on foot. Park at the *mirador;* it lies south of the road between Chipude and Igualero. Car tour 5
🚐 by bus: up to 5min on foot. Take the Valle Gran Rey bus (Timetable 19) to this viewpoint.
This is an excellent lookout for La Fortaleza (the rock shown on the cover) and into the valley below. Shade of pines.

Sea lavender
(Crithmum maritimum)

11 MIRADOR DEL SANTO

Map page 88

🚍 by car or taxi: up to 5min on foot. Park near the *mirador* (just west of Arure, signposted). Car tours 5, 6
🚐 by bus: 10-15min on foot. Take the Valle Gran Rey bus (Timetable 19) to the Arure turn-off, follow the road into the village, and then take the first track off left to the *mirador*
Breathtaking views over the isolated hamlet of Taguluche. Pines provide shade.

Andryala
cheiranthifolia

Canary bellflower
(*Canarina
canariensis*)

*Greenovia
aurea*

Aeonium nobile

*Ranunculus
cortusifolius*

Retama

13 LAS HAYAS ○

Map page 96

🚗 by car or taxi: 20-25min on foot. Park at the La Montaña Restaurant (but discreetly, lest Doña Efigenia sees you with a *picnic* lunch!). Car tours 5, 6

🚌 by bus: 20-25min on foot. Valle Gran Rey bus (Timetable 19) to La Montaña Restaurant. *Use the notes on page 97, from the 5h-point, to reach the spectacular outlook over the Gran Rey Valley. No immediate shade, but there are palms not far from this viewpoint. Allow 40min for the climb back up, if you are catching a bus.*

14 EL TION

Map page 98

🚗 by car or taxi: up to 5min on foot. Some 0.3km west of the signposted La Palmita turn-off at Las Rosas, turn south on a tarred lane: it takes you up through the village square. Keep straight up to the Amalahuigue Reservoir. Continue along the road atop the reservoir wall and then bear left, remaining on the road until it ends/becomes a track (3.3km from Las Rosas). Park here. Near Car tour 6
Picnic anywhere — there is no traffic up here. Fine view over the Vallehermoso countryside. Shade.

15 AGULO ○

Map page 99, photograph page 102

🚗 by car or taxi: 10-20min on foot. Park *well to the side of* the main road outside Agulo. Car tour 6

🚌 by bus: 10-20min on foot. Vallehermoso bus to Agulo (Timetable 20)
Choice of two picnic places; the first involves quite a climb! 1) Follow Walk 15 (page 103) to climb to views like those shown on page 102. Little shade. 2) Follow Walk 14 (page 99), and sit on the steps above the garden plots some 50m/yds beyond the end of the cobbled street, by the cemetery. From here you can admire a glorious sea-scape — with El Teide just across the sea. The only shade is near the cemetery.

16a LOS ROQUES ENAMORADOS ○

Map page 105, photograph page 108

🚗 by car or taxi: up to 5min on foot. The 'Rocks in Love' are south of Hermigua, or 2.7km north of the 3-way junction (roads to El Cedro, Hermigua and San Sebastián). Head west on this track and park at the end of it. Car tour 6

🚌 by bus: 5-10min on foot. Vallehermoso bus (Timetable 20); ask for the 'pista de tierra a Monteforte' (the track to Monteforte).

Picnic at the end of the track, with fine views over Hermigua's valley and up into the Barranco del Cedro. For a taste of the country-side and this luxuriant barranco, follow the notes on page 106 to start Walk 16; go as far as the water tank some 20-30min away. Limited shade.

Prickly poppy
(*Argemone mexicana*)

16b GARAJONAY SUMMIT

Map page 104

🚗 by car or taxi: 40min on foot. Park opposite the forestry track signposted for 'El Contadero/Garajonay'. This parking area is 1.2km north of the Igualero/Chipude road and 2.6km south of Laguna Grande. Car tour 6

Climb the forestry track (mostly in full sun) to the summit of Garajonay; keep left at any forks. At the top, it's very exposed and often windy. The viewpoint platform provides some wind protection, and a few pines offer shade. On cloudless days all of La Gomera and the other Canaries can be seen. La Fortaleza (cover photograph) is nearby.

Aeonium
manriqueorum

La Gomera's *zonas recreativas*

(See touring map of La Gomera for 🨀-symbol. All have shade, tables, benches, water; see appropriate car tour for description.)

ERMITA DE LAS NIEVES (Car tour 5)
Near Roque de Agando; barbecues

EL CEDRO (Car tour 5)

CHORROS DE EPINA (Car tour 6)

JARDIN DE LAS CRECES (Car tour 6)
Barbecues

RASO DE LA BRUMA (Car tour 6)

MERIGA (Car tour 6)
No water

LAGUNA GRANDE (Car tour 6)
Barbecues, toilets, play area, bar/restaurant

La Gomera: Short walk suggestions

Walk 6, Short walks 6-1, 6-2
Walk 8, walk from Pastrana to the Ermita de San Juán and back (access by 🚗 only)
Walk 9, Short walk 9-1 (access by 🚗 only)
Walk 10, or either of its Short walks
Walk 13, Short walk (but note steep descent; proper footwear and surefootedness required)
Walk 16, Short walk 16-2, or follow the main walk for only 20-30 minutes
Walk 17, Shorter walk 17-2

Taginaste rojo
(*Echium wildpretii*)

❈ Touring

Most people holidaying on these islands hire a car for some part of their stay. Car hire on Tenerife is quite inexpensive; rental costs on La Gomera are higher. (It pays for a group to take a hired car from Tenerife to La Gomera on the ferry.) Check the car carefully before taking it on the road, read the conditions of hire and insurance, and keep the rental firm's telephone numbers (office hours and *after closing*) with you.

The four relatively long tours described here will get you well acquainted with **Tenerife**. If your time is limited, **Tour 1 is a must**, with **Tour 4** making a good follow-up. There are two itineraries for **La Gomera**: I've simply split the island north/south. Should you have only one day there, you can combine the two, *if you make a very early start* (by hydrofoil from Tenerife).

The touring notes are brief: they contain little history or information readily available in tourist office leaflets. The facilities and 'sights' of the main towns are not described either, for the same reason. I concentrate on the 'logistics' of touring: times and distances, road conditions, and seeing places many tourists miss. Most of all, I emphasise possibilities for **walking** and **picnicking**. While some of the references to picnics 'off the beaten track' (indicated by the symbol *P* in the touring notes) may not be suitable during a long car tour, you may see a landscape that you would like to explore another day.

The large fold-out touring maps are designed to be held out opposite the touring notes and contain all the information you will need outside the towns. The tours have been written up starting from Playa de las Américas (Tenerife) and Valle Gran Rey (La Gomera)*, but they can be joined from other points quite easily. Town plans are on pages 8-9.

Remember to allow plenty of time for **visits**, and to take along **warm clothing** as well as some **food and drink**, in case you are delayed. The distances quoted in the notes are *cumulative* from the departure point. A key to the symbols is on the touring maps. **All motorists should read the country code on page 128.** *Buen viaje!*

*Most visitors stay at Valle Gran Rey; if you arrive by ferry and hire a car, join Tour 5 at San Sebastián and Tour 6 at Hermigua.

1 LAS CAÑADAS AND THE NORTHWEST

Playa de las Américas • Vilaflor • Las Cañadas • La Orotava • Puerto de la Cruz • Icod de los Vinos • Buenavista • Punta de Teno • Masca • Santiago del Teide • Los Gigantes • San Juán • Playa de las Américas

This excursion requires an early start. You may well set off in sunshine, but often the north is under cloud. In general, the roads are winding and narrow (except for the C820). Some people may find the convoluted road between Santiago and Masca vertiginous. Puerto de la Cruz and La Orotava can always be saved for another day: they are best reached via the motorways. Adeje (Picnic 1 and Walk 1) lies just off the homeward route but, as it's close to Playa de las Américas and on a good bus route, it's also best kept for another day. Reckon on 211km/131mi; 8-9 hours' driving; take Exit A from Playa de las Américas (plan page 8).

En route: ⊼ at La Caldera, Las Lajas, Las Cañadas; Picnics (see **P** symbol and pages 10-15) (1), 2, 3, 5; Walks (1), 2, 3, 5. (Other walks and picnics are described in *Landscapes of Tenerife*.)

This dramatic circuit begins on the dry rocky slopes of the south. Ascending to Las Cañadas, you head up through a forest of Canary pines — the most beautiful you'll ever see. Las Cañadas is another world, where you will cross a vast bare plateau. Fields of jagged scoria and sunken gravel 'lakes' (*cañadas*) surround you. Rich volcanic hues ooze out of the landscape. The north then greets you with the greenery of garden plots and trees; the lush Orotava Valley is a sea of rippling banana palms. Exhilarating coastal scenery takes you to the northwest and its concealed valleys. From gentle, scooped-out basins, you plunge into precipitous, fathomless ravines.

Head east along the C822 (Exit A). At the Los Cristianos junction turn off for Arona, still following the C822. Then bear left on the C511: you climb through a bleak landscape, but it is by no means

El Teide, with Montaña Blanca below to the left. Retama and Canary flaxweed brighten the highlands in spring (Car tours 1 and 2).

without beauty. Cacti and *tabaiba* flourish in this rocky terrain, and mock pepper trees grow alongside the road. Come into **Arona** (11km ♦✕⌂). The village has a charming shady church square, surrounded by balconied old houses. From up here, the mass of greenhouses on the lowlands sparkles under the sun. Hillocks of all shapes and sizes disrupt the plains.

Vineyards on walled slopes surround the TF5112 to **Vilaflor** (21km ♦▲✕⌂⊕), the highest town on the island (1161m/3810ft). Nestled on the edge of a plain, this mountain settlement looks up to the steep forested inclines that run down off the high mountain spurs above. Continue north on the C821 and soon come to Los Pinos, where Short walk 5 ends. At this lovely *mirador* (⌂), you will see some of the ancient regal Canary pines for which Vilaflor is renowned. Leaving the viewpoint, at Lomo Blanco you pass the track where Walk 5 can end and Short walk 5 begins. Then the road climbs through spectacular rugged mountain landscapes (⊓ at 27km: Las Lajas *zona recreativa,* with water and fireplaces; ⌂ at 32km).

Enter **Las Cañadas★** at the pass of **Boca de Tauce** (38km), an impressive salient of twisted rock over to the left. A spellbinding lunar landscape unfolds before you. The constant change in colour and rock formation within the encircling crater walls is the highlight of this tour and, I imagine, of your visit. Sharp-surfaced lava flows give way to smooth mounds of scoria, while sunken gravel beds create 'pools' along the floor. The majestic Teide is with you wherever

Walkers on the slopes of Montaña Blanca (the 'White Mountain'; Car tours 1 and 2)

you go, always more impressive from a distance. Bearing right at the pass, you will first skirt the immense gravel plain called Llanos de Ucanca. You may be intrigued by the bright patches of blue and green iron-containing rock in the roadside embankment, aptly called 'Los Azulejos' (The Tiles). Very soon you come to the setting shown on page 24. Stop a while at the **Parador de Las Cañadas** (45km ▲▲✕). Walk 5 starts here. Explore the 'Yellow Stones' (*P*5; photograph page 24) and 'García's Rocks', on the opposite side of the road. The latter, strange rocky upthrusts, stand guard over the eastern edge of the Ucanca Plain.

Pass by the turn-off (🚻) to the Teide funicular (you would waste most of the day queueing here) and continue on to the **Cañadas Visitors' Centre** (58km). This is an excellent source of information on the national park, with a small museum and an hourly film show. The park covers more than 720sq km and is centred round a huge crater approximately 2100m/6900ft above sea level. In spring you may see the exquisite, 2m/7ft-tall *taginaste rojo* flowering here — a magnificent sight when its tapering stem is embellished with bright red florets. Immediately beyond the visitors' centre is **El Portillo** (✕🅷WC), the 'Little Gateway'.

From here head left, descending through pines. Soon there are views over the verdant north to Puerto and the built-up coastline. Keep an eye out for the famous Margarita de Piedra (Stone Daisy), a rock formation resembling a flower, sitting back in a small *barranco* on your right. You'll pass six ICONA picnic sites (tables/benches/shade only) on this road, before you come to the signposted turn-off to **La Caldera★** (70km ✕🅷🌄 WC), a *zona recreativa* with barbecues and a play area for children in addition to the usual facilities. From this little crater *(caldera)*, there are wonderful views over the green slopes of La Orotava and the sea.

Just below the La Caldera turn-off lies the **Agua-mansa trout farm** (72km ✕WC and arboretum). From there lovely countryside scenery of tilled plots amongst sagging, lichen-covered walls and scatterings of aged chestnut trees takes you down to **La Orotava★** (85km ♦✕🚻⊕). The village is best seen during the festival of Corpus Christi (May/June), when the streets are carpeted in flowers, and in the main square intriguingly-beautiful religious 'paintings' are made from the multicoloured sands of Las Cañadas. Calle de San Francisco is the street to see, with its magnificent old mansions, lovely courtyards and wooden balconies. Also of interest: the town's principal church (La Concepción, 18th century) and the Church of San Juán, which commands a magnificent view of the surrounding valley.

Continuing on the C821 to Puerto, keep right* when you cross the bridge just outside La Orotava. If you're interested in botany (especially island flora), you might stop at the **Botanical Garden**. The compact garden is well laid out and contains a substantial collection of tropical and subtropical plants. It's on your route, some 2km south of Puerto, in the suburb of La Paz (open 09.00-19.00 (18.00 in winter).

Puerto de la Cruz★ (92km ♨▲✕➡⊕Mᴡᴄ), once a small port serving the farming town of La Orotava, is a bubbly, rather pleasant resort — as resorts go. What little remains of the old town lies buried amidst hotels and apartment blocks. Pavement gardens and flower troughs keep the town looking fresh and colourful. You may wish to visit the remains of the old port's heritage: the church of Nuestra Señora de la Peña (a typical 17th-century Spanish church), the Chapel of San Telmo (1626), the Castillo de San Felipe (small 17th-century fortress, now converted into a restaurant), and the Casa Iriarte (a charming 18th-century house, considered to be the best example of Canarian architecture in Puerto).

Leave the town on the Carretera del Norte. Joining the C820, head west for San Juán de la Rambla. Some 4km along you'll pass the museum El Castillo Parque, set back off the road on your right. The coastal road passes below cliffs towering up to the left, while breakers crash below on the right. Turn right into **San Juán** (102km), a charming, fresh-white village overlooking the sea. Las Aguas, a neighbouring hamlet on the rocky shoreline below, is a picture-postcard scene glimpsed just before San Juán. All the way from Puerto to the northwestern tip of the island, you're immersed in banana palms and roadsides bright with blooms.

Continuing along the C820, come into **Icod de los Vinos** (119km ♨▲✕➡⊕) on the fertile, vine-growing slopes below El Teide. The Church of San Marcos (16th/17th century) is worth a visit. Just below the lovely church square is Icod's famous ancient dragon trees. The nearby Playa de San Marcos is a small sandy

*If you will visit Puerto another day, turn *left* over the bridge and head west on the C820 for San Juán de la Rambla and Icod de los Vinos.

beach surrounded by dark and jagged cliffs (a 5km return detour). Leave Icod on the coastal road (TF142), passing manorial homes set amidst banana plantations.

Come into **Garachico**★ (125km ♠♙✕➍⊕). This beautifully-situated village, once an important port, was destroyed by a volcanic eruption in the early 18th century. But a few buildings of interest survive: the San Miguel Castle (16th century), the Baroque palace of the Marqués de Adeje and the Convent of San Francisco (17th century), and the Church of Santa Ana, founded in 1548 but rebuilt in 1704. Garachico is also known for its inviting natural rock pools. The Roque de Garachico, rising up off the shore, bears a cross to protect the little town from another catastrophe.

Continuing west on the TF142 (➍), the village of Buenavista is seen up ahead, resting on a fertile coastal plain, walled in by high sharp crags. Gorges and valleys cut back into this cataclysm of rock. Pass through **Buenavista** (133km ✕➍⊕) and, at the first junction, turn right and then immediately left, following the signs for the 'Faro de Teno'. Three kilometres along this road (TF1429), there are especially fine views from the **Punta del Fraile** (➌), where the island falls away into an indigo sea. The road continues to wind its way round and under rough indented cliffs, high above the sea, and then descends to the lighthouse on the dark volcanic promontory of **Punta de Teno** (141km ➌), one of the richest botanical areas in the Canaries.

From here return to Buenavista (150km) and, at the junction, turn right on the TF1426 for El Palmar. El

Laurel forests and terracing hidden in the Teno (Car tour 1)

Palmar's valley lies well hidden above the coastal plain — a steep climb up through rocky terrain covered in prickly pear, *vinagrera* and wild geraniums. The slopes are a mass of thin green lines terraced straight up to the crests (a neighbouring valley is shown in the photograph on page 21). Pass **El Palmar** (156km) and then come to fabulous views over Masca. Like the rest of the island, Masca changes with the seasons. Winter turns all the trickling falls into cascades, plunging from the heights above. Your route (which some people may find vertiginous) struggles over a dramatic landscape of deep and narrow chasms, partitioned by high cutting ridges. **Masca** (162km ✖️💽P3), the last of the valley's hamlets, is a dark cluster of dwellings sitting far below the crests on a ridge. Walk 3 explores Masca's *barranco* all the way down to the sea 600m/2000ft below, but the short version of the walk would give you a delightful introduction to the upper ravine.

From Masca, continue uphill over high squared-off peaks, coming to a viewpoint (💽P2), from where fairly easy Walk 2 would lead you to a setting similar to the one shown on pages 52-53. Then come into the sleepy village of **Santiago del Teide** (168km ♦️✖️💺⊕). Join the C820 and turn right for Los Gigantes. The landscape is again harsh, as you head through **Tamaimo** (175km 💺), an attractive village sheltering below a high rocky protrusion. From Tamaimo, turn right on the TF6281. Tomato plants now cover the landscape, as the route winds down to Los Gigantes.

At the 181km-mark, at a junction, keep right for Puerto de Santiago. **Los Gigantes** (189km ▲✖️💽) is a modern tourist complex set below sheer cliffs★ rising vertically out of the sea. Head on to tiny **Puerto de**

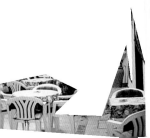

Santiago (✖️) and then join the TF6237 via the sandy beach of **La Arena**. The next village en route is tranquil **San Juán** (201km ▲✖️💺). Keep straight on along the coast, passing below Adeje (*P*1, Walk 1), to return to Playa de las Américas (211km).

Puerto de la Cruz: restaurant in a typical courtyard with Canarian balconies (Car tour 1)

2 THE CUMBRE AND THE SUN-BAKED SOUTH

Playa de las Américas • Guía de Isora • Las Cañadas • El Portillo • La Esperanza • Güimar • Arico • Granadilla • Playa de las Américas

Driving is generally good, except for some 51km of bumpy narrow road between Fasnia and Granadilla. The cumbre above Arafo is often shrouded in low-lying mists. Reckon on 232km/144mi; about 5-6 hours' driving; take Exit B from Playa de las Américas (plan page 8).

En route: ⊼ at Chio, Las Cañadas; Picnics (see **P** symbol and pages 10-15) (1), 5; Walks (1), 4, 5. (Other walks and secluded picnic settings are described in *Landscapes of Tenerife*.)

From the driest to the greenest, from the lowest to the highest, and from naked to forested — this drive gives you a taste of it all. The higher inclines along the southern flanks of the island are a dramatic contrast to the rich green slopes of the north.

Set off from Exit B in Playa de las Américas, heading north along the C822 and making for Guía de Isora. The road gradually ascends, passing below Adeje (**P**1 and Walk 1), cutting through rocky ridges and dipping into *barrancos.* There are uninterrupted views along a coastline robed in banana palms. **Guía de Isora** (22km ✕🖥⊕) is a small country town sitting high on the bare rocky slopes. Wander around the quaint narrow streets here, before setting off again.

Come into **Chio** (26km 🖥). Here turn right (C823) for Las Cañadas, coming shortly to Las Estrellas restaurant (✕ 🖭), a fine viewing point over the southwest coast. Pines begin appearing, scattered across the landscape, and smooth volcanic cones remind you of the most recent volcanic outbursts. Set amidst this scenery is the lovely Chio *zona recreativa* (⊼), with tables, benches, drinking water and barbecues. The pines subside, and you are surrounded by dark lava flows.

You enter **Las Cañadas★** at **Boca de Tauce**: continue on the C821 (🖥) along the crater floor, with the wall of peaks rising impressively alongside you. El Teide dominates the landscape, but Guajara (Tenerife's third highest mountain; photograph overleaf) projects noticeably out of the crater walls. Weird rock configurations capture your attention. The route is described in Car tour 1: pick up that tour at the 38km-point (page 18) and follow those notes as far as **El Portillo** (76km).

At El Portillo you turn off right on the C824 to climb the *cumbre.* Anthill-sized cones grow out of the inclines below the road. *Retama* (a hardy broom), white-blooming *margarita del Teide* (of the daisy family), and mauve-flowering *alhelí del Teide (Erysimum scoparium)* creep across the terrain. The tones in the gravel slopes change from maroon, purple and black, to grey, mauve and russet. **La Crucita** (89km 🚗) is the point where the pilgrims cross the C824 on their way from the north to Candelaria for the celebration of the Assumption of the Virgin of Candelaria, Tenerife's patron saint.

Pines reappear and the countryside becomes rockier and rougher. You'll snatch far reaching views along the way: a series of *miradors* follows. A detour of 1km takes you to the **Mirador de Cumbres** (🚗), looking out over the northern slopes. The **Mirador de Ortuño** (🚗) gives you fine views over the pine-robed slopes of El Teide. Finally, the **Mirador Pico de las Flores** (110km 🚗🍴) looks out over the verdant hills of La Esperanza, all the way to Santa Cruz and up to the Anaga range. Leaving the trees (and quite possibly the mist that so often envelops these summits), you come down into **La Esperanza** (116km ✕🍴), a small farming community set amidst fields and pastureland.

From La Esperanza retrace your route for 18km, then turn left to descend to the sun-bleached south via Güimar. Loose scatterings of chestnuts cover the lower slopes. The Güimar basin opens up ahead, revealing great ravines cutting deep into the escarpment (🚗 at 138km). High brown stone terraces step the slopes of

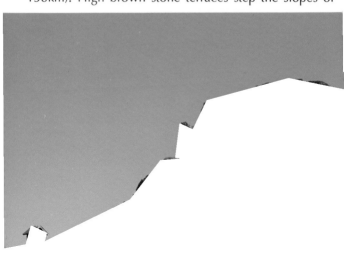

this productive agricultural centre. Vineyards abound. Bypass the centre of Arafo and go straight through **Güimar** (156km ♠✕♟⊕). Come out onto the old C822 and head towards Fasnia (signposted). Bumping along through rural scenery and winding in and out of shallow ravines, you climb out of the basin along the eastern escarpment. The **Mirador de D Martin** (162km ✕📷) offers you a final view of this great valley.

Now the monotone landscape is more harsh. Trees vanish, save for the fine-branched Jerusalem thorn bordering the roadside. In April and November its blossoms cheer up this countryside. Rock wall terraces have fortified the landscape. **Fasnia** (174km ♟) is a pleasant country village set back off the road. Between here and Arico, the landscape becomes even more bleak; there are few settlements, and the land is not cultivated. Continue via **Arico** (188km ♣✕♟) and its outposts — old Arico, new Arico, 'Arico's Ridge' (*Lomo* de Arico) and finally 'Arico's River' — **El Río de Arico**, where Walk 4 begins and ends. Approaching **Granadilla** (209km ♣✕♟), the countryside returns to cultivation. This important agricultural centre occupies one of the most fertile valleys in the south and boasts the best oranges on the island. Leaving the town, keep down to the left and follow the C614 to the motorway, then head right to Playa de las Américas (232km).

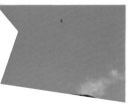

Car tours 1 and 2: The 'frowning' crown of Guajara rises above the chapel of Las Nieves ('the Snows') and the Piedras Amarillas ('Yellow Stones'; Picnic 5). The beautifully-sited Parador de Las Cañadas (not in the photograph) is just to the left of the chapel. Why not spend a night or two here? From your window, you might overlook Guajara or El Teide. This photograph was taken in August — not the best time to visit. If you come in spring, the retama bushes seen in the foreground will be a mass of bright yellow florets. In winter, Guajara's gentle slopes may be covered in snow. Walk 5 starts here.

Playa de las Américas • Tacoronte • Mesa del Mar • Bajamar • Punta del Hidalgo • Cruz del Carmen • Las Carboneras • Taborno • Pico del Inglés • La Laguna • Playa de las Américas

Some two hours of this drive are spent on the motorway, getting to and from the northeast. The descent to Mesa del Mar is down a precipitous rock face and not recommended for nervous drivers or passengers. Because of the narrow and winding roads on the Anaga Peninsula, driving will be slow. Reckon on 248km/154mi; 5-6 hours' driving; take Exit A from Playa de las Américas (plan page 8).

En route: All the walks and secluded picnic spots along this tour are described and illustrated in *Landscapes of Tenerife*, which explores the Anaga Peninsula in detail.

This short excursion visits varied landscapes. You'll drive down to the coast and take a dip in the sea-water pools (there are several choices); continue up to the summits of the Anaga and go for a stroll in the laurel forest; then perhaps finish off the day with something of historical and cultural interest, sauntering around the streets of La Laguna.

Take the motorway (Exit A) and head east. **La Candelaria★** (53km ✝▲✕⊡⊕) is a good place for a break, now or on your return. The modern basilica (1958) houses a new statue of the island's patron saint (the original statue, supposedly found by Guanche herdsmen, was lost in a tidal wave in 1826). The large square on the seafront is quite impressive, with its red-rock statues representing the ten former Guanche chiefs of Tenerife (see drawing on page 7). Continue by motorway to the El Sauzal/Tacoronte exit (7.5km beyond La Laguna), then follow signs (C820) for **Tacoronte** (88km ✝▲✕⊡⊕). Numerous miracles are attributed to the wooden statue of Christ in the 17th-century church here, and it is revered by many of the islanders.

Leave Tacoronte on the TF1221 (signposted for Valle Guerra). Some 4km along, turn down left for Mesa del Mar (signposted). At a junction 1km downhill, keep straight on. A descent past large modern houses, with gardens full of colour, brings you to the cliffs overlooking the precipitous coastline. The tourist complex of **Mesa del Mar** lies below, on jagged rocks jutting out into the sea. Superb coastal views unfold as you descend this steep, fairly hair-raising road (🚗). The complex is of little interest, but behind it, through a tunnel, you'll find a sandy beach below the cliffs.

Climb back up to the TF1221 and turn left for **Valle**

Taborno, dominated by its rock, often called the 'little Matterhorn'
(Car tour 3)

Guerra (100km ▱). From here follow signs to **Tejina** (106km ✕▱), where you join the TF121 for Bajamar. Blooming bushes and creepers, together with large banana plantations, add colour to the landscape here. Its tidal pools make **Bajamar★** (109km ▲✕▱⊕) a popular resort and swimming spot. Sharp ridges rise up behind the settlement, but plants in all shades of green soothe the dark and abrupt inclines. Continue on the same road to **Punta del Hidalgo★** (112km ▲✕⊙), once a small fishing village — until tourism discovered the spot. It lies across a slight bay with a rocky beach. Your road ends past the village at a roundabout, where high craggy crests fall away into the sea.

Return to Tejina, and from here continue on the TF121 to **Tegueste** (124km ✕▱). Tejina and Tegueste, small villages on grassy inclines, open your way to **Las Canteras** (130km), where you turn left on the TF114 and head up into the magnificent laurel forest. A *mirador* (⊙) on the right, 3km from Las Canteras, gives you captivating views of the lush green undulating hills outside La Laguna, as well as new perspectives over El Teide, Tacoronte, the small hillocks of La Esperanza, and Santa Cruz. **Cruz del Carmen★** (134km ✕⊙) is another well-designed viewpoint, framed by the forest. From here you overlook the Aguere Valley of La Laguna and have more views of the ever-present Teide.

For a brief time you leave the thick of the forest, as you drive down to the two beautifully-situated villages of Las Carboneras and Taborno. The turn-off (TF1145) is 1km past Cruz del Carmen, on your left, and sign-posted. Pass nearby the restaurant Casa Negrín (or

'Casa Carlos', ✕), and the valley opens up as you start to descend. Punta del Hidalgo reveals itself for a moment, as the coast comes into view. The Roque de Taborno (photograph page 27) is a prominent landmark, jutting high atop the ridge. **Las Carboneras**★ (142km ✕) sits fastened to a hill, skirted by cultivated plots. From here, return to the road passed earlier (TF1128) and turn left. After descending a forested ridge, you come into **Taborno**★ (147km 📷). The small dwellings of the hamlet are dispersed along the crest of the ridge, rising high above two ravines. Nestled against clumps of prickly pear, they are well sheltered from the strong winds that sweep these mountain crests.

Returning to the main road (now numbered TF1123), turn left. After 1km turn right to the **Mirador Pico del Inglés**★ (156km 📷). Perched on the spine of this range that divides the peninsula north and south, the *mirador* offers views down into the hidden cultivation of Afur's valley, and *barrancos* open up the way to the south coast and the island's guardian, El Teide.

From Pico del Inglés take the TF114 and TF121 back to **La Laguna**★ (168km ♁▲✕🚊⊕). There's much to enjoy in this charming university town. Leave La Laguna via Calle San Augustín, to return to the motorway and retrace your outgoing route to the Playas (248km).

4 BUCOLIC CHARMS OF THE RUGGED ANAGA

Playa de las Américas • La Laguna • Pico del Inglés • Roque Negro • El Bailadero • Las Bodegas • Chamorga • Taganana • Almaciga • Benijo • San Andrés • Igueste • Santa Cruz • Playa de las Américas

Some two hours of the drive are spent on motorways, getting to and from the Anaga. Driving is slow in the mountainous terrain, but the roads are not busy. Note: there are no petrol stations between the outskirts of La Laguna and San Andrés — 90km along the touring route. Reckon on 262km/162mi; about 6-7 hours' driving; take Exit A from Playa de las Américas (plan page 8).

En route: ⼞ at the Anaga Forestry Park. Walks and picnics are described in *Landscapes of Tenerife*, which explores the Anaga in detail.

This excursion takes you amidst the mountains of the Anaga. Twisting along the backbone of this range, the road is one continuous *mirador*. Inland, lost in these rugged contours, lie tiny remote villages, clinging to rocky nodules. And along the coast, quiet and secluded little bays unravel.

Start out as in Tour 3, but turn off the motorway into **La Laguna★** (80km ⼞⼞✕⼞⊕). In the town *carefully* follow signs for Las Mercedes, weaving through the narrow streets. You'll finally come out on a tree-lined road and cross the well-settled plain (⼞) of Las Mercedes. Join the TF114, soon immersing yourself in the coolness of the laurel forest. Pass the Mirador Cruz del

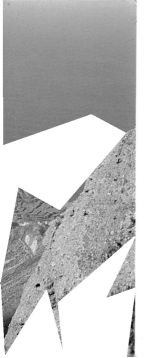

The stepped valleys of Taganana, from the Mirador El Bailadero (Car tour 4)

29

Carmen and the TF1145 to Las Carboneras (Tour 3). **Pico del Inglés**★ is your first stop. Turn right off the road to this fabulous *mirador* with its far-reaching views (91km ✕🝙). Then head back 1km and turn right on the main road (now numbered TF1123). Solitary houses speckle the ridges segmenting the isolated Afur Valley.

Some 3km along, turn left to **Roque Negro** (98km 🝙), a small, well-concealed settlement overshadowed by an enormous black basalt rock. The village square serves as a good look-out point: Afur can be seen far below in the shadows of these high crests, and the beach, the Playa del Tamadite, lies beyond the village.

From here return to the TF1123 and turn left. You will soon be looking down into the southern ravines, clothed in subtle shades of green. Fields on the higher slopes are cloaked in emerald clover. Pass a picnic site with tables (🛱) 7km from the Roque Negro turn-off. At the 108km-mark, turn off left for **El Bailadero**★ (✕🝙), the viewpoint from where the photograph on pages 28-29 was taken. Then follow this road (still the TF1123) until it ends. In 5km you'll come to the lovely **Anaga Forestry Park** and *zona recreativa* (🛱 with tables, benches, barbecues, drinking water and wc). The road is flanked by dense laurel forest all the way along. At the **Mirador de las Chamucadas** (114km 🝙), you'll have good views down to Igueste, a superbly-sited village visited later in the tour.

Descending in S-bends into open rocky terrain, your route now makes for **Las Bodegas** (119km), a hamlet sheltering in a narrow *barranco*. La Cumbrilla, on the ridge above, is more impressive in its surroundings. Jagged rocky strata emerge above the treetops along the crest. (If you don't mind bumpy roads, make a 6km return detour now to Chamorga, one of Tenerife's most beautiful villages. Barely a minute up the road from Las Bodegas, turn right, pass through a tunnel under La Cumbrilla, and head down into Chamorga. A smattering of white dwellings, the hamlet snuggles into the sides of a *barranco*, shaded by palms and loquat trees.)

The main tour returns from Las Bodegas to the Taganana turn-off, on the *left*. Some 2km up, turn left again. After 1km, you pass through a tunnel and come out overlooking the rural wonders of the Taganana. This stretch of escarpment is a landscape of razor-sharp ridges cutting down to the sea (photograph pages 28-29). **Taganana**★ (140km 🏕✕⊕), a brilliant array of white houses, is spread across the lower crests. Palms grace the gardens, making this settlement extremely photogenic. Roque de las Animas (the Ghosts' Rock), towering above the road a kilometre beyond the village, is worth a stop. Dragon trees cover the sea-side face of this mountain, but the rock colouring and vegetation camouflage this special sight from most passers-by. The roadside bars at **Playa del Roque★** (142km ✵) make a pleasant refreshment stop-off. Past **Almaciga**, **Benijo** (at the end of the road) is but a few cottages and a beach.

Returning through the tunnel, now follow the TF112 down to the southern coast, twisting and winding down the Barranco de San Andrés. From **San Andrés** (165km ✵🍹), turn left for Igueste (signposted) on the TF1121, climbing coastline cliffs. Just outside San Andrés, **Las Teresitas** (Tenerife's only white sand beach) is a touch of the tropics with its palms. You'll catch glimpses of other tiny sandy bays, barely visible from the road, as you approach **Igueste** (171km). This neat and serene village lies across the mouth of a ravine. Vegetation fills the valley, making this otherwise barren landscape fresh and green. Concrete paths cross the valley floor and disappear between the houses. Cultivated plots — well-tended groves of mangos, avocados, guavas and bananas — run down to the sea. This tremendous village setting is one of my favourites on the island.

Return along the TF1121 as far as San Andrés, from where the TF111 takes you on to **Santa Cruz** (188km ⛪🏔✵🍹⊕M). Make sure you pass through the city before (or well after) the rush hour! Then take the motorway (🍹) back to Playa de las Américas (262km).

A taste of La Gomera: Los Roques (The Rocks), with Ojila in the fore-ground (Car tour 5)

5 LA GOMERA'S SOUTHERN LANDSCAPES

Valle Gran Rey • Arure • Las Hayas • Chipude •
Alajeró • Playa de Santiago • San Sebastián • El Cedro
• Los Roques • Laguna Grande • Valle Gran Rey

This is a long drive, with several interesting stops en route. An early
start is recommended, since driving on the island's generally narrow
and sometimes rough roads will be slow. If your time is limited, El
Cedro and Los Roques can be saved for Car tour 6 — or better still,
see them on a 'walking day' (Walks 6 and 16). The El Cedro road may
be unnerving for those prone to vertigo, and is only suitable for four-
wheel-drive vehicles. Always be alert for foraging goats and sheep on
the roads — and, around settlements, for pedestrians. Note that petrol
stations en route are few and far between: Valle Gran Rey, Chipude,
Santiago and San Sebastián; some are closed Sundays. Reckon on up
to 157km/97mi, 5-6 hours' driving. Join the tour at San Sebastián, if
you come from Tenerife by ferry.

En route: ⊼ *at the Ermita de las Nieves and El Cedro; Picnics (see* **P**
symbol and pages 10-15) 6a-b, (8), 9a-b, 11, 13; Walks 6-11, 13, 16-17

You will be astonished at what this island of 378
square miles has to offer! This tour introduces you
to the south of La Gomera, which at first glance appears
bare, barren and sun-baked. For most tourists, perhaps
it is. But *you* will find valley floors laden with produce,
grassy saucer-shaped basins, elegant palm groves and
pockets of pines. The out-of-the-way beaches (stony in
winter, sandy in summer) will entice you to return for a
'beach day'. Heading back to Valle Gran Rey, you enter
another world — a salubrious forest, dark and damp
and dripping with moss. Short walks, perhaps to picnic
spots, lead you through this relic of the Tertiary Period,
to fern-drenched slopes and cascading streams. You
needn't be a walker to enjoy this rare gift of nature, but
you may become one...

Leaving Valle Gran Rey on the Vallehermoso road, a
dramatic climb takes you up the Gran Rey *barranco* —
the island's most beautiful valley. The road hangs out
over the ravine, looking out over a verdant tapestry of
palm groves, banana plots, gardens, and a streambed
filled with cane. Under 6km uphill, a roadside *mirador*
(⌖⊼) enables you to look out over neat terraced gardens. Rounding the sheer walls of the Barranco de
Arure (an adjoining valley), you come to the village of
Arure (12km ✕), set along a shallow grassy valley high
in the *cumbre*. Short walks 11-1 and 11-2 begin here. A
few remaining stone dwellings and walls preserve the
charm of the village. If you will only do this tour on La
Gomera, then don't miss the **Mirador del Santo** (⌖✝
P11): take a left at the fork just as you enter Arure and

then fork left again 0.2km further along. This viewpoint overlooks the isolated Taguluche Valley and the village of Taguluche some 500m/1650ft below. Keeping *right* at the fork, however, you pass above an enchanting reservoir and climb to the plateau, where you meander across an undulating tableland that rises up into the centre of the island. The islands of La Palma (with the twin 'humps') and El Hierro can be seen not too far in the distance. La Fortaleza, the prominent buttress of rock shown on the cover, soon steals your attention.

Coming into palm trees, you enter **Las Hayas** (17.5km ✗*P*13), the home of La Montaña Restaurant, where Doña Efigenia cooks up some of the best local dishes you'll find on the island. The setting is simple, the service is slow, the prices reasonable, and the food unforgettable. Fit it in during your stay, perhaps combining lunch with Short walk 13, which starts out here.

Leaving the village, you come to a junction at the edge of the laurel forest. Bear right for **El Cercado** (22km), the centre for ceramics. This charming village, characterised by its rustic stone cottages, sits around a cultivated basin cut up into small vegetable gardens. You look across a hillside heavily lined with stone walls on the approach to **Chipude** (24.5km ♠✗🚌⊕). Walk 10 (quite an easy walk, highly recommended for all visitors) begins here, at the church square. At the junction just outside the village, turn left (but, if you need

El Sombrero, above San Sebastián (Car tour 5)

petrol, go right here; there's a station 0.3km down the La Dama road.) La Fortaleza now dominates the landscape with its massive rock crown. Pines merge into the surrounding cloak of heather. The **Mirador del Igualero** (31km  P9b) gives you a chance to pull over and admire La Fortaleza in all its grandeur. Erquito is the meagre sprinkling of houses in the *barranco* floor far below. Walk 9 would take you down into this blissfully serene valley; tackle it, if you're *very fit!*

A short way further on, turn right for Alajeró (sign-posted) and begin a drawn-out descent to Playa de Santiago. The countryside is bare of trees and heavily smudged with rock. You peer down into sheer-sided ravines that appear without warning. Elevated tongues of land dip towards the sea, terminating abruptly in cliffs. Luminous green *tabaiba* enlivens the sombre hillsides. Then palms, dotting the inclines, announce the scattered village of **Alajeró** (40km *P*9a). From here you can do the short and easy version of Walk 9. Also note: a few villagers let rooms; enquire at the local bar. Soon you're looking across to Tenerife, made bold by the prominence of El Teide; this magnificent sight remains with you all the way to San Sebastián. Pass a turn-off left and go straight on for Santiago. Two pictur-esque hamlets, huddled up against rocky outcrops on your left (on the road you bypassed), may catch your eye as you continue the descent through a dusty and thirsty landscape, where the fields are abandoned.

Banana plantations sitting back off the sea-cliffs betray Playa de Santiago below, at the confluence of two large ravines. You enter this quiet fishing village from the west and turn left over the Barranco de Santiago. (From here you can take a 4km return detour up the east side of the *barranco:* take the next road off left; a telephone kiosk stands just inside this turn-off. This is the start of Walk 8, and non-walkers might especially enjoy this drive, to see the tucked-away hamlets of Taco, El Rumbazo and Casas de Pastrana (*P*8). These three humble settlements sit in the shadows of towering jagged walls, overlooking a valley floor crammed with gardens and orchards. This oasis of greenery is the last thing you would expect to see when you enter this initially inhospitable-looking gorge. Try the short stroll to the picnic spot, or to Benchijigua.)

The main tour continues through **Playa de Santiago** (53km ▲✕🚉⊕). This sleepy village is undergoing a 'facelift' — group tourism is on the way. Playa de Santiago boasts the best beaches and weather on the island. Day-trippers usually miss these beaches, because they lie well east of the village, embedded in the rugged coastline. A gravel track (the end of Walk 7 and only suitable for very sturdy vehicles) leads to these

Sunrise on the cumbre. You're above the sea of clouds, overlooking the laurel forest in silhouette. Tenerife lies 20km beyond, crowned by El Teide.

three glittering rocky coves, each separated by a sheer ridge projecting into the sea. You pass this track just beyond the hotel, as you start to climb out of the ravine, zigzagging up past banana groves, vineyards and avocado plots. This is the domain of Fred Olsen, the Norwegian shipping magnate. Steadily climbing, you enter a landscape carved up by impressive ravines. Razor-sharp ridges flecked with *tabaiba* separate them. Pockets of palms occupy corners of the *barrancos*. Further inland, pines, splashed in amongst *Cistus* and prickly pear, add more hues to the greenery. (If you stop for photography, pull over on *straight* stretches of road.)

Some 18km from Playa de Santiago you encounter a junction at the **Degollada de Peraza** (71km ✗☞*P*6b). Stop at the *mirador* here and look at the clean-cut Las Lajas Valley and its delightful 'stepping' reservoirs (photograph page 68). Walk 6 would take you all the way up this appealing gorge. (Two kilometres up the road to the left lies the lovely Ermita de las Nieves *zona recreativa* (🛏♂), with tables, benches, and drinking water. Steps at the side of the road alert you to this picnic site, from where there are views over the interior hills and out to Tenerife.) The main tour turns *right* at this pass, to continue through a landscape littered with stone walls. The ridges no longer burst up angrily out of the valleys. A hat-shaped rock (El Sombrero; photograph page 33), adorning a parallel ridge, steals your attention five minutes down. Then the verdure in the hillsides slowly fades out, and the landscape becomes bare, barren and sun-baked once again.

There's little to see in **San Sebastián** (87km ♨▲▲✗ ☎⊕M). Even tourism has passed it by. For those in search of history, there's the Church of the Assumption, where Columbus supposedly attended mass before setting off on his historic journey to the New World; also Columbus's house (Casa de Colón) and the simply-built Torre del Conde (Count's Tower, a 400-year-old fortress built by Felipe II). The last now houses a small museum with artefacts from La Gomera and South America, dating back to the period before the Spanish Conquest. Walks 6 and 17 end here, and Walk 7 begins here. Head for the *parador* and 'El Faro de San Cristóbal', then keep left at the fork just beyond the *parador*. Four kilometres further on, the tar ends, and you overlook the Playa de Avalo (✗), a secluded, stony beach, opening out from a *barranco* bed sprinkled with

Beautifully-coloured rock formations rise above the Playa del Inglés, near Valle Gran Rey.

date palms and tamarix shrubs. (Those with four-wheel-drive vehicles may like to continue all the way down, just under 3km further on.)

Return to the *parador* and turn right up the island's largest valley, the Barranco de la Villa. As you ascend, the wide valley floor closes up into a narrow V. Sharply-outlined ridges drip down off the *barranco* walls. Closer to the *cumbre,* the craggy slopes are greener. Keep an eye open for the large clumps of *candelabra* on the inclines above. Some 9km up from San Sebastián, a *mirador* (📷) affords another view over the reservoirs in the Barranco de Las Lajas, with garden plots below them. In winter this valley comes to life, when the streams are full, and water cascades over the reservoir walls. The road curls its way up the *barranco.* Scarred cliffs tower above. Leaving the south behind, you pass the Los Cumbres Restaurant (✖) and soon duck into a long tunnel. Emerging on the north side of the island, a completely different landscape confronts you: heather and strands of laurel forest cap the summits and trail down the upper inclines. Sheer dome-shaped peaks stand shoulder-to-shoulder over on the right. The countryside is fresher and more grassy. A parking place beside an abandoned restaurant a few hundred metres beyond the tunnel exit enables you to pull over and enjoy this sudden change of scene. You get a taste of the north — of Car tour 6. Your views encompass the banana plantations of Hermigua below.

A kilometre further on (114km), turn left for El Cedro, heading up into the **Garajonay National Park★**. This amazing, well-engineered road snakes up the precipitous wooded slopes of the *cumbre.* Springs trickle down out of the mossy banks. Houseleeks of different shapes and sizes speckle the rock faces and white-to-carmine-coloured flowers (*Senecio*) fleck the shady banks. Lichen-clad heather and moss-covered laurels shade the route. You can feel the dampness the forest generates. For much of the year, the *cumbre* lies shrouded in mist, which has a special beauty all its own. When you come to the turn-off right for **El Cedro** (signposted), don't miss this scenic spot. The forestry track to the hamlet is *only recommended for four-wheel drive* vehicles: keep right at the junction mid-way down. On foot, use the notes for Short walk 16-2 on page 106 to visit the hamlet and go on to the fairy-tale forest and picnic area (♦⋤; with tables, benches and drinking water).

Returning from El Cedro and mounting the crest of the *cumbre*, you soon encounter a junction, the **Cruz de la Zarcita** (126.5km; photograph below), where Short walk 6-1 begins. Turn left: you come to the intriguing place where four enormous pillars of lava (the remains of volcanic chimneys) burst up out of the landscape, **Los Roques★** (📷*P*6a). The viewing plat-form on the right overlooks Roque de Agando, a massive protrusion growing straight out of the sweeping Barranco de Benchijigua. El Teide rises in the background, beyond the finely-etched ravines of La Villa and Las Lajas. Another balcony, on the left-hand side of the road, looks out onto the stouter rocks of Ojila, Zarcita and Carmen (from left to right; photograph page 31).

Roque de la Zarcita, in the foreground, attempts to mimic El Teide, rising in the distance above clouds. The photograph was taken from Cruz de la Zarcita (Car tours 5, 6).

Return to Cruz de la Zarcita and turn left. Just after you remount the *cumbre,* be sure to pull over and take in the panorama over the immense, reclining Barranco de Benchijigua, on the south side of the ridge (Walk 8; photograph page 74). Remaining on the *cumbre,* continue straight on past the Chipude junction, making for **Laguna Grande** (✕🛏; Car tour 6). You'll catch a glimpse of El Cedro ensconced in the wooded valley below and, shortly, Tenerife will be in full view — often with El Teide piercing the mantle of cloud that hovers over the islands. The track to the summit of Garajonay branches off left some 1.2km further on (Car tour 6.) A wing of pine trees runs down off the mountain, fraying out as it enters the heath-tree vegetation zone.

Keep left at the next two junctions, but bear right at the third, to return to Valle Gran Rey (about 157km) via **Las Hayas** (✕) and your outgoing route.

Descending into this grand valley at sunset, you find the *barranco* in another mood: its austere façade is softer, and the walls no longer frown down upon you. If you haven't fallen in love with La Gomera by now, you never will.

Valle Gran Rey • Las Hayas • Laguna Grande • Hermigua • Agulo • Garajonay National Park Visitors' Centre • Vallehermoso • Arure • Valle Gran Rey

The roads are winding, and there are some rough patches: driving will be slow. Watch out for foraging goats and sheep on the roads, and for pedestrians in the villages. There are only three petrol stations en route: at Valle Gran Rey, Hermigua and Vallehermoso. Reckon on 104km/65mi; 4-5 hours' driving. If you come by ferry to San Sebastián, join (and leave) the tour at the Hermigua/El Cedro junction: head north up the Barranco de la Villa and, after 17km, bear right for Hermigua. Pick up the tour at 39km and follow it to, then from, Arure.

En route: ♨ at Chorros de Epina, (Meriga), (Jardín de las Creces), (Raso de la Bruma), Laguna Grande; *P* (see pages 10-15) 13, (14), 15, 16a, 16b; Walks 11-17

The perfect way to begin this drive is to catch a sunrise from atop Garajonay. The majestic beauty of El Teide, in rapidly changing hues of gold, orange and mauve, afloat on a sea of white clouds, is a sight you'll long remember (see page 34). If you're not an early bird, the sunset is often equally rewarding. On this tour you delve into the rugged north, where narrow ravines carve up the countryside. The hillsides, patched in scrub and capped with woods, are discernibly greener than in the south. Banana palms, orchards and garden plots fill the streambeds, intensifying the greenery. Tall palms gracefully ornament picturesque villages. But alas, all too frequently a cape of cloud descends before midday — another good reason for an early start.

Follow Tour 5 as far as the junction just beyond **Las Hayas** (18km). Here keep straight on (left) and, when you come to a T-junction, bear right. Crossing the rolling hills of the island's centre, you thread your way through heather and laurel. Pine woods appear in the background. Pass the sunken *zona recreativa* of **Laguna Grande** (23km ✕♨), with tables and benches, drinking water, and barbecues. The excellent restaurant here, with its cosy fireplace, is worth keeping in mind, in case you hit one of the really cold spells that the island sometimes saves up for visitors. A meal here will set you up for any drop in the temperature!

In the laurel forest

If it's a fine day, you'll want to climb **Garajonay** to enjoy the extensive views it offers. The turn-off is 2.6km beyond Laguna Grande: pull into the large parking area on your left and climb the signposted track opposite. It takes about half an hour to reach the summit; keep left at any forks. Ascending, you look across pine trees to the imposing rock shown on the cover, La Fortaleza. As the name suggests, the rock resembles a fortress. On clear days, the view from this peak (*P*16b) encompasses El Hierro, La Palma, Tenerife and Gran Canaria.

Continuing to Hermigua, you enjoy more superb views off the *cumbre,* on either side of this backbone of the island. Keep left at the Santiago/Los Roques junction and twist down through the laurel forest. You come to the north road at **Cruz de la Zarcita** (30.5km); turn left. (But if you're not doing Tour 5, first continue ahead to see Los Roques★, described on page 38.) Plump peaks, all in a line, rise abruptly up out of the valley over to your right, and a stream bounces down the *barranco* floor into a large and tranquil reservoir. Pass the forestry track to El Cedro (see Tour 5, page 38). Then, some 2.7km beyond the San Sebastián junction, take the first track off to the left to the **Roques Enamorados** (*P*16a; photograph page 108). From here you can sample the delights of the Barranco del Cedro — the lushest gorge on the island. Follow Walk 16 for 20 to 30 minutes.

Hermigua (43km ▲✕🛱⊕♣M) is a striking contrast of white houses and green banana groves. Hamlets step corners of the ravine walls and stretch along the floor. Fruit trees grow amidst the houses. Walk 15 ends here; Walks 16 and 17 begin here. Two places you might like to visit are the private museum in Las Telares (small collection of traditional household utensils) and the old Dominican Convent further along the road.

As you leave Hermigua, turn off right for its beach, circling the Piloto Pension and Restaurant. Once over the bridge, veer left along the track. A natural rock pool sits at the beach here, with its back to a sheer wall of rock that runs straight into the sea — a tremendous setting. (*Note:* The best and safest swimming on the island is on the south coast. The north is often rough and can be extremely dangerous: even the pool here is safe *only* when the sea is *dead calm!*)

Leaving this valley, you see Tenerife sitting across the water straight in front of you. Then, climbing high above the sea, you round a corner and look over what has to be the most beautifully situated village on the island. **Agulo** (51km ♨ and ✕ evenings only) is set in an alcove of rocky cliffs, high above the sea, looking straight out towards El Teide — a view much envied by other villages (**P**15; photograph page 102). The bakery here *(dulcería)*, next door to the artesan's shop at the entrance to the village, is well known for its *típico* cakes and biscuits. My favourite is the *torta de cuajada,* a small cake made with goats' cheese, but it's only obtainable in the winter. Wander along the cobbled alleys that pass through the banana groves and admire the archetypal houses that give this village so much character. Walks 14 and 15 start here.

The tunnel shown in the photograph on page 102 leads you out of Agulo's natural amphitheatre of cliffs into a deep, sheer-faced ravine. Rock walls rise above you. Reaching the upper confines of this *barranco*, you come to **Las Rosas** (56km ✕), a farming village of scattered houses. Fork left on a narrow road signposted for La Palmita; it takes you up to the **Garajonay National Park Visitors' Centre★** (59km). Walkers and nature enthusiasts alike will find a wealth of information here. Walk 14 (another strenuous hike, I'm sorry to say) passes this way. There's a typical Canarian dwelling to be seen, as well as local handicrafts, a film about the National Park ... and even a *cafetería* — which puts it two up on Tenerife's Cañadas Visitors' Centre!

Return to the junction in Las Rosas and bear left. (After 0.3km you could take a 6.5km return detour to an out of the way lookout and picnic spot (**P**14) — well worth the effort on fine days. Turn up the steep bumpy lane that climbs to the square in Las Rosas. Continue straight up through the square to the Amalahuigue Reservoir. Cross the reservoir wall and then veer left, remaining on the road all the way up. You climb a scruffy shallow ravine as far as the tree-line. Simple dwellings sit off the road. You need go no further than where the tar ends — on the crest of the ridge. From here, a vast cauldron stretches across in front of you, and ridges pour down into it. Shortly before the tar ends, you have a fine view of Roque Cano, the massive lava pillar shown on page 101.)

The main tour continues towards Vallehermoso. You look down into plunging ravines that drop off into the sea. Terraced vineyards ladder the slopes. Swinging inland, you wind around large open valleys, passing above the pretty village of Tamagarda, noted for its typical oblong houses, all with tiled rooftops and either brown or grey woodwork. Palms adorn the hillsides, and Roque Cano (photograph page 101) bursts upon the scene: sitting like an exclamation mark, it punctuates the end of a trailing ridge.

Another tunnel takes you into the cauldron, and you're engulfed by hills. Roque Cano looms overhead. The farming settlement of **Vallehermoso** (70km ▲✕ ⊞⊕) soon unfolds, tucked up against the valley walls. Dust-brown slopes climb back off it. A stream of banana plots, fruit trees and gardens flows down the valley floor, reviving the landscape. My strongest recollection of this village is the *miel de palma* — palm honey. It's made by boiling the palm sap and leaving it to cool into a black syrup. Try this mouth-watering recipe: mix *gofio* (roasted maize flour; see page 77) and the honey (as much as you like) into a doughy mixture, add pieces of white cheese *(queso blanco),* lemon rind, and ground almonds ... and life will never be the same again! Sample the good local wine and the *mistela,* a local liqueur. Two kilometres north of the village lies the Playa de Vallehermoso. Please note: this beach is extremely dangerous at *all* times, hence the swimming pool nearby, which is only filled in summer. Some tourist books and brochures say that this is a good beach, but obviously no one has survived to tell otherwise! However, the setting is wonderful. Walk 12 is located in this area (see photograph pages 90-91).

From here head back to your starting point, leaving the village at the right and circling above it. Climbing out of the valley, its bucolic charm becomes more evident. You look out over its adjoining valleys, laced with palms. Plots of potatoes and tomatoes sit squeezed along the *barranco* floors and into the gentler pauses in the walls. The striking hamlet of Macayo captures your attention adorning the nose of a palm-studded ridge on your left, its simple stone dwellings clinging to the side of the ridge. Restaurante La Romantica, 7.5km up from Vallehermoso, is the ideal place from which to survey this enchanting hamlet.

Approaching the summits, the countryside is scruffier, with scrub running down the declining ridges. In spring the route is splashed with resplendent yellow-flowering *codéso.* At the 83km-mark, you pass the

Alojera/Taguluche turn-off. These isolated villages rest amongst dry, denuded hills, completely cut off by the cloud-catching *cumbre*. This scene will have much more impact from the Mirador del Santo later in the tour.

In the meantime, just around the corner, you come to the Restaurant Los Chorros de Epina (✖🍽). Just beyond it, turn into a track branching off to the spring of the same name, now a picnic site maintained by ICONA (🛏♁). Stop here to stretch your legs and admire the exquisite hamlet of Epina: follow the path off to the right (on the restaurant side of the track). Some minutes along, behind the chapel above the picnic area, you'll stumble onto a habitat of the precious pink-flowering Canary geranium, and shortly thereafter you will be looking through the trees onto Epina, a neat little hamlet resting at the foot of the escarpment amidst green garden plots — a sharp contrast to the bleached hills below. The picnic site provides tables and benches set in 'balconies', and the wonderful spring splashes out sweet water.

Leaving the Chorros de Epina, keep zigzagging uphill in the company of El Teide. Your vista sweeps back across the gently-declining coastal hills and over the numerous gulleys segmenting the great cauldron. Heath trees, growing out of cracks in the rock, lean out over the road. You disappear into the forest. At the Arure/La Laguna junction (the first you encounter), turn right. (A left turn would lead to two ICONA picnic sites, located in a wonderful stretch of forest — Raso de la Bruma and Jardín de las Creces; Walk 13.)

Leaving the forest, descend to **Arure** (91km ✖), the home of a delicious honey. Some quaint stone cottages rest alongside the garden plots lining the *barranco* floor. At the end of the village (0.2km before the Valle Gran Rey junction), branch off right to the **Mirador del Santo** (🍽♁*P*11), unless you stopped there earlier in the day. This superb *mirador* hangs out from the escarpment, high above Taguluche, a remote pocket of civilisation sitting deep in a bare landscape ruptured by upheavals of sharply eroded hills. The escarpment curving around on either side of you frames this magnificent view.

Heading home, make for Valle Gran Rey along your outgoing route (104km). Or, if it's not too late in the day, why not head for Doña Efigenia's La Montaña Restaurant at Las Hayas (5km away) and try one of her *gofio y verdura* (roasted maize and vegetables) dishes?

 Walking

This book describes five walks reached quite easily from a base in the **south of Tenerife**, but I've emphasised walking on **La Gomera**. (The companion volume, *Landscapes of Tenerife,* covers fifty-five long and short walks on that island — on the Teno and Anaga peninsulas, in the Orotava Valley, and around Las Cañadas.)

There are walks in this book for everyone.

Beginners: Don't be discouraged by the 'strenuous' rating given to most of the walks in the book. Start out by looking over the Picnicking section — there you'll find four suggestions for Tenerife and twelve for La Gomera. These are just right for short and easy walks. Further suggestions for short walks are on pages 12 (Tenerife) and 15 (La Gomera). On La Gomera you can also explore ICONA's nature trails: a leaflet is available at the Centro de Visitantes at Garajonay National Park.

Experienced walkers: If you are used to rough terrain and have a head for heights, you should be able to tackle all the walks in this book — taking into account, of course, the season and weather conditions. For example, in rainy weather some of the walks will be unsuitable, especially the Barranco de Masca, the lower Barranco del Río, and walks in the north of La Gomera.

Regarding **grading of the walks**: I have written up the walks on La Gomera with the bus timetables in mind. This means that several walks *ascend* inland and are thus graded as 'very strenuous'. These require good stamina and are only recommended for the hardy. Nevertheless, all walks can be done in the reverse direction *(descending),* simply by following the very detailed large-scale maps. Moreover, the longer walks can be cut in half. Thus most of the walks, in some permutation, are accessible to everyone ... your only problems being transport and aching legs — if you tackle a walk with a very steep descent before getting used to the terrain.

Regarding **transport on La Gomera**: The average walker (see under 'Walking times' below) will find it impossible to get to and return from walks by public transport. You will have to do much shorter walks, or rely on a taxi or friends to take you to the start of a walk or collect you. If you are spending enough time on La Gomera, it is also worth identifying places where you can leave a hired car just off the main roads, *near a bus route*. While this is not always possible, you may find that you can drive to your starting point early in the morning, walk, and then catch a bus back to the car.

Walking times are given for reaching certain points, based on an average walking rate of 3-4km/h and allowing an extra 20 minutes for each 100m/330ft of ascent. *Really fit* hikers will complete these walks in half the time and should have few problems using the buses to come and go, even on La Gomera.

Caution is needed regarding the terrain and the weather. Some of the walks cross very remote country and can be both *very cold and potentially hazardous.* Distances on these islands can be very deceptive, with exhausting descents into and ascents out of hidden *barrancos* between you and your goal. Only link up walks by using the notes in the book or by following roads or tracks indicated on the walking maps. *Don't attempt to cross unmapped terrain; always be prepared for bad weather, and always walk with friends.*

G uides, waymarking, maps

Should you wish to hire a **guide**, enquire at the tourist offices, the visitors' centres at the national parks, or at the islands' *paradores*. Some hotels on Tenerife also organise walking tours: ask your hotel porter, or look in the local tourist newspapers and magazines.

Many walks on both islands are **waymarked**, usually with paint splashes or small cairns. These waymarks are mostly referred to in the text. But please do not presume that the walks described in this book *always* follow the waymarked routes: *they do not!*

The **maps** in this book have been heavily adapted from the 1:25,000 or 1:50,000 military maps of the islands. You can purchase these in advance of your visit from your usual map supplier, or buy them on the islands. But do remember that, while they are very useful for contours and heights, they do not show many of the paths I've located for you. Moreover, some of the paths that they *do* show are now no longer viable.

D ogs — and other nuisances

There are few nuisances to worry the walker on either Tenerife or La Gomera. The **dogs** tend to *look*

more vicious than they really are — especially the
shepherds' dogs. Nevertheless, you may wish to invest
in an ultrasonic dog deterrent; for information, write to
Dazer UK, 51 Alfriston Road, London SW11 6NR.

Hunters blasting away with their shotguns may occa-
sionally scare the wits out of you, especially in the
more remote country areas, and especially on Tenerife.

You'll be happy to know that there are *no* poisonous
snakes or insects on either island.

Weather
Island weather is often unpredictable, but there
are a few signs and weather patterns that may help you
forecast a walking day. Tenerife and La Gomera share
much the same weather. Both are blessed with good
walking weather all year round.

The north unfortunately has more than its fair share of
rain, but boasts pleasant temperatures. The south soaks
up the sun. Las Américas/Los Cristianos on Tenerife and
Playa de Santiago on La Gomera enjoy the best weather.
On La Gomera, Valle Gran Rey is slightly cooler and is
prone to strong winds. Wind also strikes the southern
coastline east of Los Cristianos, but rain is rare. During
the winter months, the north not only suffers from
clouds, but often experiences very strong winds, especially on the more open hilltops. Walking and keeping
upright at the same time can be a problem!

Apart from the seasons, the **weather patterns** are in-
fluenced by two main **winds**: the *alisio*, the trade wind
from the northeast, and the *tiempo del sur,* an easterly
or southeasterly wind. The trade wind is identified by
the low-flying fluffy clouds which hover over the north
(between 600-1500m/2000-5000ft) for much of the
year. On Tenerife, you can head to Las Cañadas to get
above the clouds and enjoy clear blue skies. But on La
Gomera, the *cumbre* (central mountain chain) and
Garajonay usually remain deep in cloud — not much
fun for walking, since it's cold and wet, with zero
visibility. The walks in the north of La Gomera all
disappear into cloud at some stage. Sometimes, however, the summits sit just above the sea of clouds, and
you have the wonderful sight shown on pages 34-35.

The *tiempo del sur,* quite different, brings heat and
dust. Temperatures rise considerably, and the atmos-
phere is filled with very fine dust particles. This weather
is more frequent in winter than in summer. It seldom

lasts more than three or four days. These days, outside of summer, are good for walking; even if it's a little warm, the sky is cloudless, although a bit hazy. (In summer it is *not* advisable to walk when the *tiempo del sur* is blowing; you risk sunstroke and dehydration, unless you are in a very shaded area.)

Two less frequent winds that could spoil your day are the nor'westerly from the North Atlantic and the sou'westerly from the tropics. Both bring heavy rains. This weather covers the entire island and can last a few days. When these winds blow in winter, Las Cañadas and El Teide are more likely to see snow than rain.

Remember (especially in winter) that no matter how wonderfully the day begins, it could deteriorate. **Always be prepared for the worst.** Along Gomera's *cumbre* the weather is less predictable still, and it can be ***exceedingly cold.*** Remember too, that the sun can be your enemy, perhaps especially on days of light cloud cover.

What to take

If you buy this book on one of the islands, and you haven't brought any special equipment such as a rucksack or walking boots, you can still do some of the walks, or buy yourself some equipment at one of the sports shops. Don't attempt the more difficult walks without the proper gear. For each walk in the book, the *minimum* equipment is listed. Where walking boots are required, there is, unfortunately, no substitute: you will need to rely on the grip and ankle support they provide, as well as their waterproof qualities. All other walks should be made with stout lace-up shoes with thick rubber soles, to grip on wet or slippery surfaces.

You may find the following checklist useful:

walking boots (which must be broken-in and comfortable)	up-to-date bus timetable
	small rucksack
waterproof rain gear (outside summer months)	plastic bottle with water-purifying tablets
long-sleeved shirt (sun protection)	long trousers, tight at the ankles
first-aid kit, including bandages	insect repellent
plastic plates, cups, etc	knives and openers
anorak (zip opening)	2 lightweight cardigans
map (see page 46)	extra pair of socks
spare bootlaces	plastic groundsheet
sunhat, sunglasses, suncream	torch, whistle, compass

Please bear in mind that I've not done *every* walk in this book under *all* weather conditions. Use good judgement to modify my equipment lists according to the season.

Organisation of the walks

The walks in this book are located in the south of Tenerife and all over La Gomera. I hope that the book is set out so that you can plan your walks easily, depending on how far you want to go, your abilities and equipment, and — to some extent — the season.

You might begin by considering the large touring maps between pages 16 and 17. Here you can see at a glance the overall terrain, main and secondary roads, and the orientation of the walking maps that accompany the text. Flipping through the book, you'll see that there is at least one photograph for every walk.

Having selected one or two potential excursions from the map and the photographs, turn to the relevant walk. At the top of the page you will find planning information: distance/time, grade, equipment, and how to get there by bus. If the grade and equipment specifications are beyond your scope, don't despair! *There's almost always a short or alternative version of a walk,* and in most cases these are far less demanding of agility and equipment. If even these seem too tough, then turn to the Picnicking section on pages 10-15, for a good selection of really short, easy walks.

When you are on your walk, you will find that the text begins with an introduction to the overall landscape and then quickly turns to a detailed description of the route itself. The large-scale maps (1:40,000) have been specially annotated and, where possible, set out facing the walking notes. Times are given for reaching certain points in the walk (*important:* see 'Walking times', page 46). *Do* compare your own times with those in the book on one or two short walks, before you set off on a long hike. Remember that I've included only *minimal stops* at viewpoints; allow ample extra time for photography, picnicking, or swimming.

Below is a key to the symbols on the walking maps:

▓▓▓	correspond to roads and tracks on the touring maps	→	direction: main walk	♠	woodland; national park boundary
		⇨	alternative	✝/✚	church/cemetery, shrine
		🔁	best views		
▬▬	track	∧∧	rock formations	□□□	village, habitations
- - - -	path, steps	∩/‖	cave/gate, barrier	■	specified building
▬▬▬	main walk	🚗	car parking	∮	pylon, wires
⚊⚊⚊	alternative	🚌	bus stop	◆→	spring, tank, etc
⚊⚊⚊	watercourse				
⋯500⋯	altitude	P	picnics (see pages 10-15)	🪑	picnic site with tables
⚡	danger! vertigo!				

1 ADEJE • BARRANCO DEL INFIERNO • ADEJE

Distance: 8km/5mi; 4h

Grade: moderate climb/descent of 300m/1000ft; some agility required; the *barranco* may be impassable after heavy rain.

Equipment: stout shoes or walking boots, sunhat, cardigan, anorak, picnic, water

How to get there/return: 🚌 or 🚐 (Timetables 7, 10) to/from Adeje. (By car, you can park near the path into the *barranco*, saving 30min.)

The Barranco del Infierno (Hell's Valley) is probably the most walked ravine in the Canaries. So early in the morning is the quietest time for this ramble. This *barranco* boasts one of the few permanent streams on Tenerife. High sheer walls close in on you as you make your way up the defile of jagged rock. Wild blackberry drapes itself over the trees and bushes, and ivy 'tunnels' convey you up to the splendid falls. Adeje is an immaculate village, with an appealing combination of old and new, set at the foot of the ragged crags that house the deep chasm of Hell's Valley.

Start the walk by climbing the main, tree-lined street in Adeje. At the top of the rise, turn left at the junction. Not far ahead, bear right (signposted 'Barranco del Infierno'). At the end of this street (**30min**; limited car parking), just beyond the last house on the right, find your signposted path. Soon you're looking into the ravine. At this point it's dry: further up the *barranco*, the water has been diverted for irrigation into watercourses and pipes. Clumps of prickly pear, *valo* bushes and *tabaiba* coat the steep slopes, and white *margarita* grows alongside the path.

At around **1h** you find yourself walking along a small *canal*. A minute along, you cross it and then continue above it (Picnic 1). Several minutes later, at a fork, keep right. A few moments later cross the watercourse again via a concrete culvert. Then veer right and zigzag down a gravelly path to the streambed, which you cross. A couple of minutes further on, cross the streambed again. A brief ascent brings you back to the *canal*. Continue down to your right until you reach the streambed again. You'll notice a small dam built across the stream,

Near Picnic 1: pools in the Barranco del Infierno

Adeje, from the sun-parched Barranco del Infierno (Picnic 1)

slightly above you. Make for it and continue at the left-hand side of the dam wall, then bear right on a path.

From here on the walk requires a bit more agility, but this is the most beautiful part of the hike. When the path branches, some two minutes from the dam, keep left along the stream, which is soon gurgling alongside you. Some willows spread out along the floor. Your first stream crossing comes up quickly, and for the rest of the walk you criss-cross the stream, in places plunging through bushes and ferns. Pools become more frequent, and you will see and hear many birds. Close to the end of the passable section of the ravine, a soft mossy rock face, dripping with water, is seen, and you reach the lovely three-tiered waterfall through a narrow dark defile (**2h15min**). It splashes down some 80m/250ft into a small pool. The *barranco* walls tower 1000m/3300ft above you here, blocking out the sky.

Return from the falls, remembering to turn left on leaving the streambed below the dam: head back down the streambed; don't follow the *canal*. The bus leaves from the roundabout on the left at the end of the tree-lined street in Adeje (**4h**).

Copyright © Sunflower Books

2 ARASA • LA CABEZADA • (FINCA DE GUERGUES) • ARASA

Distance: 6km/3.7mi; 3h

Grade: easy-moderate, with ascents/descents of some 200m/650ft overall; **possibility of vertigo** (for one minute only)

Equipment: stout shoes or walking boots, sunhat, cardigan, raingear anorak, picnic, water

How to get there and return: 🚌 to the Arasa *mirador* (it lies on the only track branching west off the TF1427 between Santiago del Teide and Masca), or 🚐 to Playa de San Juán (Timetable 10) and taxi to the *mirador*. Leave your transport where the track forks. Arrange for the taxi to collect you in time for your return bus from Playa de San Juán.

Here's an opportunity to taste the pleasures of the Masca Valley, without the slog — or hazards — of Walk 3! This hike offers spectacular views as you wind along a high jagged neck of land. *Barrancos* fall away on either side, hundreds of metres below. On the left lies the Barranco Seco, its slopes carpeted in shades of green; on the right the Barranco de Masca is concealed below precipitous walls.

Start out at the fork in the track at Arasa (Picnic 2), where you leave your transport. After admiring the view from the *mirador,* follow the other track over to the abandoned hamlet, crossing a stream on the way. A couple of minutes allows you sufficient time to see this beautifully-sheltered enclosure. Return to where you entered the hamlet and take the path heading down into a gulley. Three minutes down into the gulley, leave the path and cross the stream (by a partly-collapsed cone-like construction of mud and stone). Once across, follow the small trail heading round the bottom of the rocky slope, passing below a vertical rock wall. For a moment the path fades, but it soon reappears below the crest — sometimes stone-paved. Beyond a stone wall (about **30min**) faded red dots on the rocks mark your route on nearly every turning.

This old threshing floor at Los Pajares is edged by candelabra and tabaiba. The photograph was taken looking east, over the Barranco Seco, towards El Teide.

52

As you cross the terrain, the colour becomes bolder: pinks, mauves, yellows and maroons vie with the golden broom and glossy-green *tabaiba*. You will keep wanting to stop, to peer over the edge of the ridge and down into the Masca *barranco*, to enjoy the different textures that the slopes on the other side gradually reveal under the moving sun.

Soon you are enjoying continuous views down into *both* ravines, as you stride along on the backbone of the ridge. Clinging to the slope, the path dips across a narrow neck of rock. Slowly, the coastline unravels: Los Gigantes, Playa de las Américas, and Los Cristianos are impressive sights. A table-topped mountain sits on the far horizon.

At **1h10min** the terrain drops away abruptly, and some people might find this short (10m/yds) stretch of path unnerving. The views over Masca's valley are superb. But the rough, sharp peak your path ascends blocks out everything else for the moment, leaving you in anticipation about what lies ahead. Then — the least expected sight: green terraced slopes, stepped with rocks. A couple of stone huts nestle on the hillside. It's quite an exhilarating sight. The faded dots lead you down to them, as the path fades.

You reach the stone huts, La Cabezada, at **1h20min**. A large circular stone construction sits below this old

Light and shade in the depths of Masca's barranco (Walk 3)

farm; once it was used for threshing the wheat and barley that was grown here. Its simple design makes it very impressive. Flat stones pave it and rocks enclose it. This perch sits amongst boulders and commands breathtaking views of the rest of this upheaval of basalt. Solitude. Only a few birds twitter and goats bleat in the distance. La Gomera is clearly visible.

More stone dwellings can be spotted, blending into the landscape further downhill: the farms of Los Pajares (shown on pages 52-53) and Guerges. If you wish to visit these settlements, the path lies directly below the threshing site you're on — add an hour or more for this detour, not included in the main walk.

On the return journey, continue to seek out the faded red paint splashes. With the sun on the upcoming slope, the green-leafed *tabaiba* brightens the landscape, and the ridge over to your right is no longer dulled by shadows. You should be back at your waiting transport at Arasa in about **3h**.

3 MASCA • BARRANCO DE MASCA • PLAYA DE MASCA • MASCA

Distance: 9km/5.6mi; 7-8h   **Photograph opposite**

Grade: very strenuous, potentially hazardous descent/ascent of 600m/1950ft; *recommended only for expert walkers.* **Possibility of vertigo**

Equipment: walking boots, sunhat, raingear, cardigan, anorak, whistle, water, picnic

How to get there and return: 🚌 to Masca or 🚐 to Playa de San Juán (Timetable 10) and taxi to Masca; arrange for the taxi to collect you for your return bus connection from Playa de San Juán.

Short walk: Masca — wooden bridge — Masca (2km/1.3mi; 1h30min; moderate; stout shoes will suffice). Follow the main walk for just under 1h and return the same way.

Alternative walks

1 Masca — Playa de Masca (4.5km/2.8mi; 3h30min; grade and equipment as above). 🚐 to Playa de San Juán and taxi to Masca. Arrange at Los Gigantes for the Masca cruise boat to collect you at the bottom of the gorge (see page 58).

2 Barranco de Masca from Playa de Masca (stout shoes required). 🛥 cruise (*book in advance*) from Los Gigantes to Masca beach; return sailing four hours later. Walk *up* the gorge as far as you like.

T he Barranco de Masca lies hidden in the huge block of roughly-dissected basalt that covers the north-western corner of the island. The *barranco* drops from

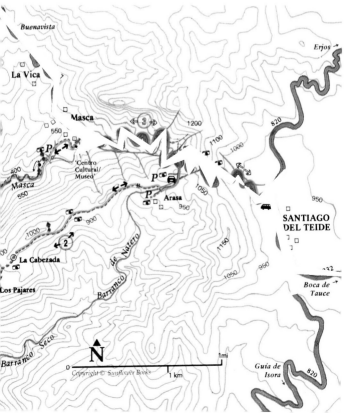

the hamlet of old Masca (600m/1950ft) to the sea below. Sheer jagged walls — in places only metres apart — rise above a boulder-crammed floor, leaving only just enough space for the surefooted walker to squeeze through (see photograph page 54).

The walk starts in old Masca, below the newer settlement. This well-tended, authentic little village is a favourite spot for many Canarians. Little has changed here since the completion of the road in the late 1970s. Quaint stone cottages stand on either side of a neatly cobbled path. Tiny flower beds and many species of cacti cheer the way. Make your way downhill to a house bearing the words 'Centro Cultural/Museo'. Just past this building, on the right, a small wooden cross on the edge of a wide path marks your turn-off for the gorge. Here, a well-used path goes right, but you turn *left*. Head down past a few cottages.

From here on, just follow the faded yellow dots which mark your route. Once beyond the houses the path becomes obscure as it climbs over bare rock. Keep to the bare rock, facing La Vica, and bits of the path will reveal themselves. Your way keeps to the left side of the cultivation — you never actually enter it. Everything imaginable seems to grow in this lush green valley. The descent over loose stones can be slow and slippery, but eventually you reach a stream. Two enormous boulders serve as landmarks here: head down to the left of the boulders, following the streambed.

You come out onto a rocky ledge (Picnic 3). Just below it is a bridge you must cross (**1h**). *Attention: check for loose boards as you cross. If not crossed with extra care, this bridge can be dangerous!* (An overhead wire makes crossing a bit easier.) Once over the bridge, continue up left for a short time and then swing right. A water tank sits below. From now on, the constant sound of running water accompanies you ... and some stretches of vertiginous path await you.

The gulley narrows. Dark patterned naked rock dominates the left side of the gorge. When you reach the stream again, scramble across it. The gorge walls tower above you here, and cascading pools keep the air wonderfully fresh. Cross the stream again several minutes later, where Indian cane has taken up residence in patches along the floor. One more stream crossing comes up not long afterwards, and then you're in the depths of the *barranco*. Keep left alongside the stream. Shortly, the streambed widens out, where streams and gorges meet. A low concrete wall has been built across the confluence. This very picturesque spot is reached in about **2h**.

At this point, the *barranco* becomes a narrow shaded chasm and veers left, heading for the sea. A thin *canal* (watercourse) is built into the left-hand wall of the gorge. Descend the dam-like wall on the left. Cross the river and, from here on, you can't possibly lose your way. Your best markers are small cairns and large yellow paint splashes indicating stream crossings and climbing points. To reach the beach from here takes about another 90 minutes' clambering over rocks and boulders, occasional wading (depending on rainfall and irrigation requirements) and climbing up old, crumbled paths. The indented walls rise precipitously — in some places as high as 800m/2600ft. Gashes and gaping holes scar the walls, and several side-gorges give the Masca ravine 'arms'.

At about **2h20min** your way passes under a rock. The *barranco* becomes an extended series of S-curves. When in doubt about the path, stop and look for those piles of stones and yellow dots. If there has been rain recently, the way may *seem* impassable at about **2h50min**. Here, **caution is needed.** The best way down is alongside the cascading water on your left. Make sure your feet are secure and your hands find good places to grip. Just after, look out for an interesting rock arch up on your left.

At **3h** an enormous *barranco* branches off to the right. An unexpected sight is unveiled minutes later, on your own path: some neatly terraced plots rise up above the stream on the left. Your first thought is: who in the world could they belong to? Then the path winds up over these plots (note: the path is broken at the outset). You reach a rocky crest and see the sea — at long last! And a building. Immediately the feeling of isolation is shattered.

The path remains high above the stream and heads towards a large recess in the wall — the local residence for goats. To reach the beach, follow the wall down to the stream and continue down the streambed until you come to the sea. The building (a private house) is by no means an eyesore: its rock construction blends with the landscape, and the large rubber trees on the property add to the greenery of the valley.

Carnival on Tenerife

In about **3h30min** you will be on the beach. It's an intriguing, serene spot, accessible only on foot or by boat. Even the possibility of finding local fishermen here is remote. Boats sometimes break the mood, as they whizz in for a quick look and then whizz out again. The cruise boat from Los Gigantes brings day-trippers to the beach and returns for them four hours later. It will also pick up walkers who have descended the gorge for the *one-way* trip back to Los Gigantes; you will not be left stranded if you have booked in advance and you arrive in time for the return sailing (an early morning start is recommended).

The beach is rocky and swimming from it is difficult, but a walkway takes you several metres/yards out into the sea, where a large rock makes an ideal spot for swimming and picnicking. Refresh yourself for the uphill slog back to Masca (**7-8h**).

From the Barranco del Río, you look down the central spine — over the coast and towards Gran Canaria.

4 BARRANCO DEL RIO (UPPER SECTION)

See also lower photograph opposite

Distance: 22km/13.6mi; 10h

Grade: strenuous climb/descent of 1100m (3600ft); **possibility of vertigo**

Equipment: stout shoes or walking boots, cardigan, anorak, raingear, sunhat, picnic, water

How to get there and return: 🚌 or 🚐 (Timetables 6, 9) to El Río de Arico

Short walk: El Río — *barranco* overlook — El Río (6km/3.7mi; 2h30min; easy-moderate; equipment as above). Follow the main walk to the farm buildings (1h30min); return the same way.

Alternative walk: Barranco del Río (lower section; 18km/11.2mi; 10h; *expert,* with an ascent/descent of 600m/2000ft; **danger of vertigo**; walking boots, whistle essential). See description on page 61.

The Barranco del Río is another of the many great gorges that cut into the mountainous backbone of Tenerife. An unrelenting climb up bleak, windswept (especially in winter) slopes brings you to the edge of the higher elevations of the gorge. This bewitching landscape, with its isolated farmlands and solitary stone buildings, will linger in your mind for days afterwards.

Decided to go? Then **start out** by following the street at the left of the church square in El Río. You'll come onto a forestry track beyond the last houses. A first landmark, a couple of old farm buildings overlooking the whole escarpment below, comes at about **1h30min**. *The Short walk returns from here.* There are few plots up here, as the terrain becomes more harsh and rocky. The undulating southern plain spreads out below, with small hillocks, water tanks, and greenhouses.

At about **2h** you'll come to the turn-off into the lower *barranco. The Alternative walk bears left here.* Your route continues straight up the rough track, passing the house shown on page 61 at about **2h30min**. There are no turn-offs on this tiring climb, so enjoy the splendid views, including Gran Canaria.

At under **5h** meet the track coming in from Izaña: turn left on it, down into the *barranco.* Almost at once you come to one of the most spectacular sights on the walk, where the chasm opens like a wide crack in the earth. Two-three minutes from here watch for a cairn on your left, and bear left on a path down into the *barranco.* When the path fades, a couple of minutes downhill, turn left: another path will take you down onto a level path within a minute or two. Keep right here, and follow this path down to the *barranco* floor. Just before reaching the streambed, the route may prove

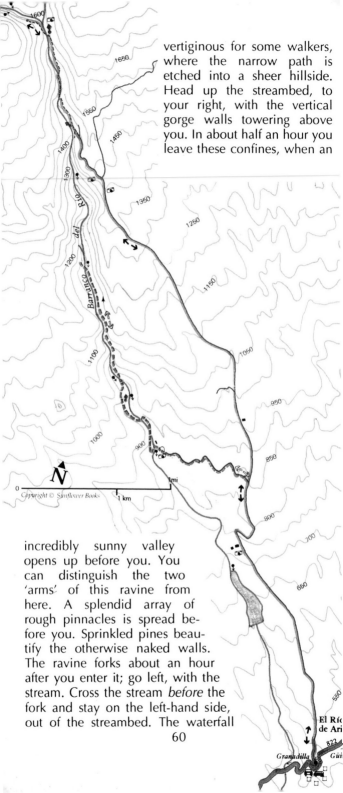

vertiginous for some walkers, where the narrow path is etched into a sheer hillside. Head up the streambed, to your right, with the vertical gorge walls towering above you. In about half an hour you leave these confines, when an

incredibly sunny valley opens up before you. You can distinguish the two 'arms' of this ravine from here. A splendid array of rough pinnacles is spread before you. Sprinkled pines beautify the otherwise naked walls. The ravine forks about an hour after you enter it; go left, with the stream. Cross the stream *before* the fork and stay on the left-hand side, out of the streambed. The waterfall discloses itself under 20 minutes later, tumbling through a crevice near an old water gallery (**6h30min**).

Once out of the *barranco,* your return hike is quite easy, with time to enjoy the views you were too busy huffing and puffing to appreciate earlier (**10h**).

Alternative walk (only recommended for *experts*)

Follow the main walk for 2h, then turn left on the track towards the lower *barranco.* When the track ends, a tunnel sits straight across from you, as you look into a small depression. Keeping right, cross this depression and head over to the tunnel on an overgrown path. Enter the tunnel by clambering over a fence of rocks and branches. Out of the tunnel two minutes later, you are in the lower confines of the *barranco.* What a sight! The deep, narrow ravine falls away on both sides. A wide path heads into this great cleft, hugging the wall on your right. Bushes and rubble attempt to block your way.

A couple of goats' shelters in the side of the embankment lie at the end of your path. The last of these has a wall. You descend into the gorge from below this shelter. Parts of the path have crumbled away, and scrambling is necessary before you can pick up the continuation. As the path slips and slides its way down the side of the gorge, it swings right and then winds steeply down to an old abandoned water gallery, just above the streambed. Another minute or so of pushing your way through *tabaiba* bushes brings you out onto the floor of the ravine. This rocky streambed is now your route.

Head right, up the gorge, clambering over rocks and stones. The pale brown walls rise vertically above you, reaching up about 70m/230ft. At about 3h30min a (seasonal) waterfall blocks the way. Fifty metres/yards before it, take the small path on the left to round this obstacle. This section of path is vertiginous, and caution is needed for the next 10 minutes' climbing, until you reach an open area. Here you cross the stream, as another cascade blocks your way a little further up. This is a most beautiful spot, with a prickly pear 'orchard' in grassy confines set above pools in the streambed. Once again, you must climb over rock to continue up the ravine.

Eventually the *barranco* sides close in on you, as you head up a narrow passageway of rock. Come out amidst boulders and pools. Not far in front of you, a lone pine rises. From here, keep below and to the left of the pine. You can either follow the streambed or a small path on the right of the stream. End the outward walk at the water gallery: you're there in about 5h20min.

Allow about the same time for your return (**10h**).

Climbing the Barranco del Río (Walk 4)

5 PARADOR DE LAS CAÑADAS • PAISAJE LUNAR • VILAFLOR

Distance: 26km/16mi; 8h   **See also photograph pages 24-25**

Grade: quite strenuous: ascent of 350m/1150ft and (sometimes slippery) descent of 850m/2800ft. Agility and a good sense of direction are required: route-finding is very difficult on the approach to the Paisaje Lunar if waymarking has not been renewed, and the descent to the 'moon landscape' is a scramble on all fours.

Equipment: stout shoes or walking boots, sunhat, cardigan, gloves, anorak, raingear, picnic, water

How to get there: 🚌 to the Parador de las Cañadas (Timetable 4)
To return: 🚌 from Lomo Blanco or Vilaflor (Timetables 4, 5)

Short walk: Lomo Blanco — watercourse — Mirador de los Pinos (15km/9.3mi; 4h; moderate; equipment as above). 🚌 (Timetable 4) to Lomo Blanco, where a rough gravel track leads to Madre del Agua. Follow this road for about 2h, or until until you hear gushing water. Picnic by the watercourse, under the shade of a pleasant eucalyptus tree, and return by the same route, this time continuing downhill on the C821 to the lovely Mirador de los Pinos, where you can pick up the same bus on its afternoon return to Vilaflor and the Playas.

Constantly-changing landscapes are encountered on this long hike: the stark splendour of Las Cañadas; the sprawling black-sand slopes of Montaña de las Arenas; the sandstone moulds of the Paisaje Lunar; and the forest of old Canary pines. The real Canary pine is the noble among peasants, and the pines of Vilaflor are renowned for their grandeur. Paisaje Lunar (the 'Moon Landscape'; see below) is the focal point of the walk: soft creams, beiges, yellows, browns and greys saturate its smooth conical formations. And you'll find, on the trek towards Vilaflor, that the southern crater walls are as spectacular as the interior, northern rock faces.

Paisaje Lunar — the 'Moon Landscape'

Start out at the *parador*. Head for the main road, past the chapel, and turn left (south). After 50m/yds along the main road, meet a gravel track on your left. Follow it until it fades (**10min**). Veer right alongside the rocky ridge and then follow a line of loosely-spaced rocks for a few minutes, to a tarred road. Turn left and, within a minute, you pass through the control barrier into the Las Cañadas track. The fascinating formation of pink and yellow rocks shown on pages 24-25 rises just in front of you. The mellow colours give this fine natural sculpture its name — Piedras Amarillas ('Yellow Stones'; Picnic 5). At the **35min**-mark you pass through a *cañada* (gravel plain). Here Guajara — the bastion of the encircling walls — is seen at its best, rising 500m/1640ft from the crater floor. Splashes of yellow lichen, like paint daubs, decorate the higher rock faces. In spring, *taginaste rojo* — which may grow to 3m/10ft — add bold strokes of red to this canvas.

Your ascent begins at the **1h**-mark. *Attention:* it's not very obvious. It lies not far beyond a turn-off to the left, and about 70m/yds past a bend in the track dominated by a towering wall of rock. Your only landmark is a small cairn on the right-hand side of the track. Turn up right. The path is clear and easy to follow. At **1h40min**, you reach the edge of the crater at the Degollada (Pass) de Guajara (2373m/7785ft). The views are magnificent. The tones are the most dramatic aspect of this landscape, as they flow into and across each other. A metal pole and various signs on rocks mark this pass.

Ignore the small path branching off right at the pass: a red arrow shows the way, beneath bleached pumice cliffs on the right. Gran Canaria seems surprisingly close from this vantage point. At **1h55min**, after a brief ascent, the path forks: a red arrow points right (to Guajara) and a white one left indicates your route to Vilaflor. There may also be a metal pole here. Barely a minute down from the turn-off, the path forks: keep right. Yellow dots and white arrows constantly indicate the route (the arrows are for those coming *from* Vilaflor). The coastal plain is seen far below, and over to your right — still in the distance — is Montaña de las Arenas, with its charred sides and maroon summit. At the foot of this sandhill lies a patch of black sand, encircled by pines. The route makes for this point. Below you, a gulley has roughly carved its way down the slope. Pines, full of character, dot this landscape.

The path, a dry watercourse, turns down a low side-ridge and begins to zigzag straight downhill. Although the route is vague, put your faith in the dots: you can't go wrong, as long as you head down the crest. A large pine, quite a way down on the right (just above a small gulley), is a good landmark: make for it. From this tree (**2h50min**), make your way down to the rolling hillock of fine, gravelly black sand. A line of loosely-spaced rocks guides you downhill. About 20 minutes from the tree (**3h10min**) come to a metal pole. A minute further downhill, slightly to the right, there *should* be another pole, with a sign 'Paisaje Lunar' — indicating a viewpoint on the right. Only parts of the 'moon landscape' can be seen from this viewpoint, but the gulley cradling it is quite impressive all the same.

Continue down, guided by the line of rocks. Keep an eye open for a large rock on your right; it bears a faded yellow dot. Take the faint path not far below this rock, heading *left* across the slope.* Your path hugs the steep incline as it cuts across the line of rocks (**3h20min**). A few minutes later the path bends round and you re-cross the line of rocks. Before reaching the edge of the gorge, you pass a large pine with another waymarking dot. To get down to the Paisaje Lunar you have to scramble down a steep rock face (on all fours). Watch for any waymarking. As you approach the bottom, you'll be ploughing through thick, loose soil. At **3h40min**, the incline evens out and you're overlooking a gulley. Keep along the edge of this gulley and in a minute or so you will be above the Paisaje Lunar, where smooth eroded fingers of pumice, in soft pastel tones, 'grow' out of the gorge walls. Now *slide* down the gravelly rock-face to get there. A lone pine marks your entry point. Unfortunately, once you are down

*If you cannot find this path, continue beside the line of stones until you meet a faint path crossing your route and bear *right* along it.

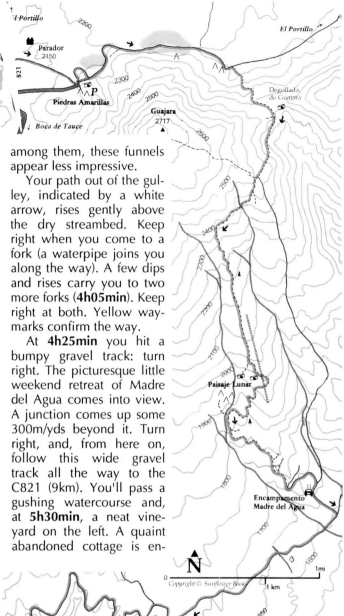

among them, these funnels appear less impressive.

Your path out of the gulley, indicated by a white arrow, rises gently above the dry streambed. Keep right when you come to a fork (a waterpipe joins you along the way). A few dips and rises carry you to two more forks (**4h05min**). Keep right at both. Yellow waymarks confirm the way.

At **4h25min** you hit a bumpy gravel track: turn right. The picturesque little weekend retreat of Madre del Agua comes into view. A junction comes up some 300m/yds beyond it. Turn right, and, from here on, follow this wide gravel track all the way to the C821 (9km). You'll pass a gushing watercourse and, at **5h30min**, a neat vineyard on the left. A quaint abandoned cottage is en-

countered at **6h30min**. Tall pines lead you out to the main road at Lomo Blanco at **7h15min**. You can catch the El Portillo bus here if you made an early morning start (by car or taxi); if not, descend via the lovely Mirador de los Pinos to Vilaflor (**8h**).

65

6 LOMO FRAGOSO • LA LAJA • ROQUE DE AGANDO • SAN SEBASTIAN

See also photograph page 33   NB: Map begins on pages 68-69

Distance: 22km/13.6mi; 8h

Grade: strenuous ascent of 850m/2800ft, followed by a descent of 1050m/3450ft

Equipment: stout shoes or walking boots, sunhat, cardigan, anorak, raingear, long trousers, picnic, water

How to get there: 🚌 to San Sebastián (Timetables 19-21) and taxi from there to the first reservoir at Lomo Fragoso (Bar Teresa)

To return: 🚌 from San Sebastián (Timetables 19-21)

Short walks

1 Cruz de la Zarcita — Roque de Agando — La Laja — Lomo Fragoso (10km/6.2mi; 3h; easy-moderate descent of 1000m/3300ft). Take the Valle Gran Rey 🚌 (Timetable 19) to Cruz de la Zarcita (the junction above Roque de Agando). Walk down the road: just past Roque de Agando, a signpost at the left of the road indicates the Garajonay National Park. Follow the path behind the sign, using the map page 68; this is very straightforward. Note that the start of the walk can be very cold and wet: be prepared! To return to San Sebastián, telephone for a taxi from the Bar Teresa at Lomo Fragoso.

2 Degollada de Peraza — Ayamosna — San Sebastián (10.5km/6.5mi; 3h; easy-moderate descent of 950m/3100ft). Take the Playa de Santiago 🚌 to the Degollada de Peraza (Timetable 21) and pick up the main walk at the 5h-point.

Alternative walk: Lomo Fragoso — La Laja — Degollada de Peraza — Ayamosna — San Sebastián (18km/11.2mi; 6h50min; strenuous ascent of 750m/2450ft, followed by a descent of 950m/3100ft; access as main walk). Follow the main walk for 1h40min. Then branch left on a faint path (marked with a finger post) and climb to the Degollada de Peraza (ignore forks off to the left). This takes about 2h10min, and you rejoin the main walk route at the 5h-point.

A kaleidoscope of natural beauty awaits the rambler on this hike. It will cost you a little energy, but the rewards will be ample. The first steps of the walk lead you up past the coffee-brown (English coffee, that is) reservoirs of the Lajas Valley, four lakelets that step their way back up the *barranco*. Palm trees and freshly-cultivated plots enhance this tropical setting. Weaving in and out of narrow gulleys, you climb amidst sparse pines. In winter cascades and waterfalls enliven the normally-dry streambeds. The ascent ends by Roque de Agando (photograph page 74), a giant swollen finger of rock that bursts up out of an already-dramatic landscape. Home is all downhill, with corners of curiosity, sweeping panoramas, and wide-open countryside.

Your taxi drops you at the first reservoir, the Embalse de Llano de la Villa. The pretty hamlet of Lomo Fragoso sits across the water, fastened to a rock face. **Start out** by continuing up the road. Cross a bridge below the

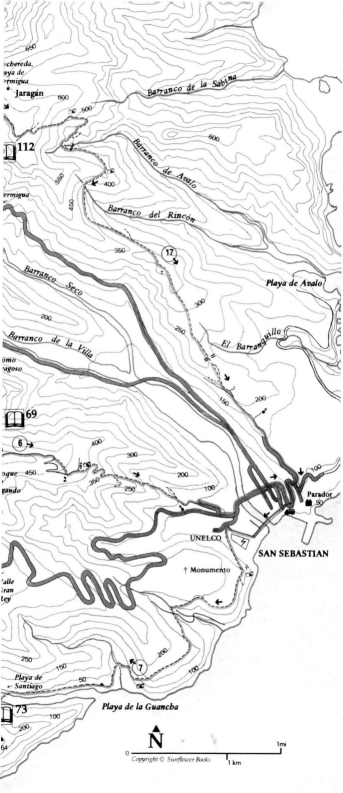

chereda,
ya de
rmigua
Jaragán

650

600

500

112

550

rmigua

450

400

Barranco de la Sabina

600

Barranco de Avalo

Barranco del Rincón

350

17

Playa de Avalo

300

Barranco Seco

200

250

El Barranquillo

Barranco de la Villa

150

200

omo
ragoso

69

6

100

oque 450

400

300

200

200

gando

350

250

250

100

Parador

50

UNELCO

SAN SEBASTIAN

Valle
Gran
Rey

† Monumento

250

150

200

7

100

50

Playa de
Santiago

73

100

200

64

Playa de la Guancha

N

0   1mi

Copyright © Sunflower Books   1 km

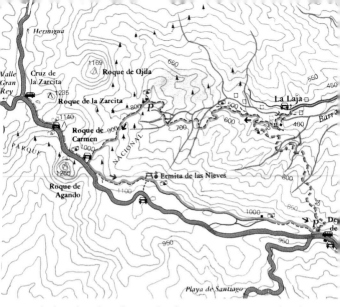

Embalse de Chejelipes, the largest reservoir. After heavy rains, great sheets of water tumble over these walls, bounding on down the valley floor. Heading up into the Barranco de Las Lajas, you pass the hamlet of Chejelipes, a peaceful haven with a sizeable foreign community. Beyond the reservoirs, you're looking down into a healthy stream. Soon Los Roques come into view, high up in the *barranco.*

La Laja slowly introduces itself (**1h20min**), and plots shelve the streambed. Here you leave the road: turn left down a path that takes you across the streambed (an electricity substation stands across the road from this path). Almost at once, veer right and cross a small bridge. Climb up past abandoned houses, ignoring two faint branch-offs to the right. Blue paint marks lead you

The Izcagüe and Chejelipes reservoirs in the Barranco de las Lajas

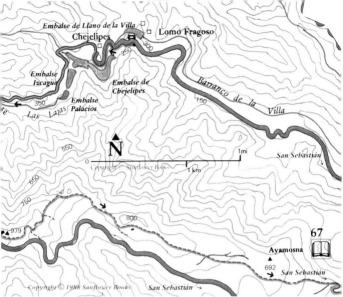

along your route. The way swings sharply right, just below an inhabited house. At the fork immediately beyond the house, continue straight ahead over the small *barranco* and scramble up the ridge opposite. Half a dozen dwellings rest on the nose of this ridge: once you've passed them and crossed the ridge, you pick up a clear path rounding the hillside. Weather permitting, you may get a brilliant view of El Teide in the distance. A few minutes over the ridge, pass a faint path branching off left (**1h40min**). *(The Alternative walk heads left here.)* Continue straight ahead for several minutes, to a fork: head left, and you'll be looking down onto a handful of rustic dwellings. The neatly-paved path zigzags up into the pine zone; some red paint splashes mark the way. (Ignore the fork down to the right.) At about **2h15min** cross the streambed; four more crossings will follow before you come to an enchanting forestry house with a verandah, on a crest at the edge of the wood (**3h**; Picnic 6a). From here there is a stupendous view of Los Roques: (from left to right) Agando, Carmen, La Zarcita and Ojila. These great lava pillars (shown on pages 31, 38-39, 74 and 111) are the remains of volcanic chimneys — lava that solidified inside volcanic vents.

To make for Roque de Agando, continue up the spine of the ridge (don't take the path heading behind the forestry house). On the ascent a wonderful panorama of the faded green valleys below is revealed. Tenerife sits in the background, clearly outlined. The road and the *mirador* are reached in under **4h**. Go left

69

along the road for a few minutes, then turn off left on a path for the Ermita de las Nieves (description page 36); keep left at a fork.

From the *ermita* take the track downhill but, at a fork, head left *uphill* on a faint track. Another track joins from the right (beyond a burned-out house). Don't miss the magnificent views down into the Barranco de Las Lajas from the edge of the escarpment here, but be careful if it's windy! The entire start of the hike is revealed. Just past this viewpoint, another immense U-shaped *barranco* on the right overlooks the south coast. When the track fizzles out, head straight downhill on a very steep path, which quickly drops you down onto the road near the Mirador Degollada de Peraza (**5h**; Picnic 6b). From here you can see the reservoirs at the start of the walk, now just small khaki-coloured pools.

Not far past the nearby bar, leave the road, heading left on a gravel track. Immediately behind a shed built of concrete blocks, branch off right on a faint, disused track (blocked off by rocks). When this track begins descending towards the road again, bear left on a wide paved path (just beneath an overhead cable). This was once a well-travelled route to San Sebastián, and much of it is still superbly intact. Ignore all branch-offs. Looking down the valley, a fascinating hillside wrinkled with terracing catches your attention. This setting is shown on page 33: a hat-shaped rock ('El Sombrero') balances atop a crest. When you round the ravine, there's a good outlook over the Barranco de la Villa. Keep left at the fork shortly after.

At **6h30min** you're passing the pastoral outpost of Ayamosna (*beware:* you may enounter unchained dogs here), and then a track becomes your way (you can cut off a corner not far above a farmstead). Just before a row of houses, take a path off to the right. At a fork shortly after, veer *left,* on a narrow path. Joining a path coming in from the left, you come onto a track (by a water tank). It takes you to a road on the outskirts of town. A few minutes down the road turn right to the Valle Gran Rey road, then bear left to San Sebastián (**8h**).

7 SAN SEBASTIAN • PLAYA DE LA GUANCHA • EL CABRITO • PLAYA DE SANTIAGO

Distance: 20.5km/12.7mi; 9h   **Map begins on page 67**

Grade: very strenuous ascents/descents of 1150m/3800ft overall, on stony, sometimes hard-to-find paths

Equipment: stout shoes or walking boots, sunhat, cardigan, raingear, swimwear, picnic, plenty of water

How to get there: 🚌 to San Sebastián (Timetables 19-21)
To return: 🚌 from Playa de Santiago (Timetable 21)

Short walk: San Sebastián — Playa de la Guancha — San Sebastián (10km/6.2mi; 3h20min; moderate ascents/descents of 400m/1300ft overall; access and equipment as above). Follow the main walk for 1h40min and return the same way.

U p at the crack of dawn, you'll catch the sun rising and perhaps see the morning ferry trailing across to Tenerife. Then, struggling in and out of *barrancos,* you'll cross a barren landscape strewn with rock, where ravines narrow into shady fissures. At the mouth of one of these sits the tiny outpost of El Cabrito — an oasis of greenery only accessible by boat or on foot.

Setting out from town, follow the road running southwest along the beach front. Near the end of the road, turn off right and head along to UNELCO (the town power plant). Just past the power plant entrance, go left on the gravelly path running alongside the enclosure. (Note: the beachfront is about to be 'tarted up'. When this happens, make your way to the power station and start the walk there.) A few minutes uphill finds you on the remains of an old cobbled path, here and there

Descending to Playa de la Guancha, set at the foot of jagged cliffs

marked by splashes of paint and arrows. Passing over the first ridge, you'll see a wooden cross below (though it may have toppled over). On the slopes high above stands the great Sacred Heart Monument. Some 20 minutes up, keep right at a fork (away from the cliffs).

At the **1h**-mark you cross the streambed and scramble straight up the other side. Then cross a dirt track, clamber up an embankment, and rejoin your path. You cross another ridge and catch sight of Playa del Cabrito, set deep in the sheer coastline ahead, and then Playa de la Guancha directly below. It's a lonely beach, set in a

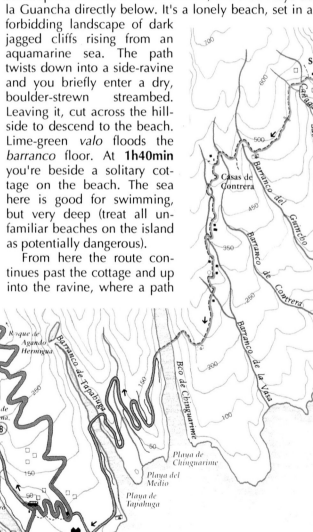

forbidding landscape of dark jagged cliffs rising from an aquamarine sea. The path twists down into a side-ravine and you briefly enter a dry, boulder-strewn streambed. Leaving it, cut across the hillside to descend to the beach. Lime-green *valo* floods the *barranco* floor. At **1h40min** you're beside a solitary cottage on the beach. The sea here is good for swimming, but very deep (treat all unfamiliar beaches on the island as potentially dangerous).

From here the route continues past the cottage and up into the ravine, where a path reveals itself. Now the paint waymarkers come into their own: together with small cairns, they'll help to keep you on the path, as you enter and leave the streambed from time to time. About half an hour from the beach the way swings left across the *barranco,* and the climb begins. The route is hard to find until you reach the ravine walls: aim initially for the faint white arrow on a rock just above the streambed. Higher up, watch for paint waymarks and the remains of the old path, when the route fades again. On reaching the crest, an exhilarating sight greets you: you look straight

down into a deep ravine. Knurls, resembling steep stairways, tumble down into it. To the left you spot a tiny Garden of Eden — El Cabrito. The full beauty of this verdant outpost is revealed a little further on, when you look down on its banana groves, fruit trees and vegetable plots neatly embroidering the *barranco* floor.

Making for El Cabrito, head up left and swing across the sheer side of the ridge. A steep, gravelly path drops you down into the *barranco.* The El Cabrito *finca* (formerly a croft) sits behind a thick stone wall (**3h 20min**). Remember that this is private property; don't climb the wall or attempt to enter the farm. Follow the track to the long stony beach and turn right, continuing along the shore on the track (a wire may be stretched across this track, but you can scramble round the 'gatepost' on the left). Nearer the quay, the track disappears into the plantation. As it veers right, keep below the cliffs on a path. The path forks left and you pass under a large fig tree. Some 100m/yds uphill come to a row of houses and swing back left. Above some plots, the way appears to continue to the right, but in fact veers *left*. At a T-junction several minutes later, continue uphill on a steep path and reach a flat crest (**4h**). Four identical crests lie ahead of you. Follow the crest inland and scramble over a dyke. Several minutes later be sure to fork left off the main path. You enter a watercourse and leave it on a faint trail that curves to the left. As you pass over bare rock, find your continuation ahead (beside the streak of cream and maroon rock).

At **5h** Santiago is glimpsed, and then the abandoned hamlet of Seima, superbly located in open countryside overlooking the sea. The path leads you there (**5h 20min**) and to a junction: immediately after the first cluster of buildings, turn left downhill on a faint path that crosses the *barranco*, from where the path becomes clearer. After clambering over a natural 'wall' of broken rock, you see the Casas de Contrera, an old farmstead two *barrancos* away (keep straight at the fork when climbing out of the first *barranco* and, when the path fades out as you approach the second one, find your continuation on the opposite side before descending).

At the abandoned Casas de Contrera (**6h30min**) your onward path begins behind the wooden cross and the furthest stone buildings: here descend to the left, crossing a dry streambed. Re-cross almost at once. When you return to the crest, the paint waymarks are less frequent. Below farm buildings, ignore the path coming in from the left; pick up the streambed again: cross it and pass three stone houses. Beyond the third, go to the left of a threshing floor. A trail lies just below:

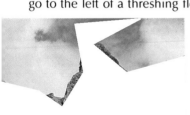

follow it to the right, then go downhill beside a watercourse, towards a stone building. Slide down a steep gravelly path (200m/650ft) into tomato plots and banana groves and scramble over boulders to a gravel track (**7h 30min**). Now more tiring ups and downs take you to Playa de Santiago after another 90 minutes (**9h**).

Roque de Agando, seen from Walk 8

8 BARRANCO DE SANTIAGO • BENCHIJIGUA • IMADA • ALAJERO JUNCTION

Distance: 17km; 10.5mi; 8h   **See photograph opposite**

Grade: strenuous, with an overall ascent of 1400m/4600ft

Equipment: stout shoes or walking boots, sunhat, cardigan, anorak, long trousers, raingear, picnic, plenty of water

How to get there: 🚌 to Santiago (Timetable 21)

To return: 🚌 from the Alajeró junction to San Sebastián (Timetable 21)

Short walk: Imada — Barranco de Guarimiar — Playa de Santiago (8.5km/5.3mi; 3h; easy-moderate descent of 900m/2950ft, but *not recommended for beginners* because of a short stretch of vertiginous path, which is dangerous when wet). Taxi to Imada or bus to the Alajeró junction (Timetable 21) and start there. Notes page 76.

Alternative walks

1 Santiago — Lomo del Gato — Santiago (14km/8.7mi; 4h40min; moderate climb/descent of 450m/1475ft; equipment/access as main walk). Follow the main walk for 2h40min and return the same way.

2 Barranco de Santiago — Benchijigua — Imada — Barranco de Guarimiar — Santiago (23km/14.3mi; 9h15min; strenuous, with overall ascent/descent of 950m/3100ft; *recommended for experienced hikers only*). Follow the main walk to Imada, then see page 76.

The Barranco de Santiago is not one of those 'love at first sight' ravines. But beyond its stark and inhospitable façade, the most unexpected sight greets you — a boulder-strewn floor crammed with gardens and orchards. Small hamlets and graceful palms decorate the valley walls. In winter a stream adds to the beauty. Deeper in the hills, weird and wonderful rocks burst out of the landscape.

Leave the Playa de Santiago bus at the first cluster of houses inside the *barranco*. (The bus stops just where a road leads up into this ravine; a public telephone stands just inside the road.) Refer to the map on *page 72* to **start out:** follow this road, with the ravine walls on your right. By **1h** the *barranco* has sprung to life: gardens shelter amidst clumps of wild cane and, if you're lucky, the stream is a babbling brook. A chuckling *canal* and palms rustling in the breeze greet you.

Some **1h20min** from Santiago (beyond the second road turning off left) the route forks; the ravine likewise. Head right on the gravel track, up into a valley graced with yellow-flowering mimosa and teeming with palms. Just before the track ends, head right uphill on the first turn-off you come to — a rocky path climbing up through an uncultivated strip of hillside. You reach a higher track and the pretty hamlet of Pastrana; turn left. A few minutes along, just before the track ends, take a path branching off left. Soon, looking over the stream-

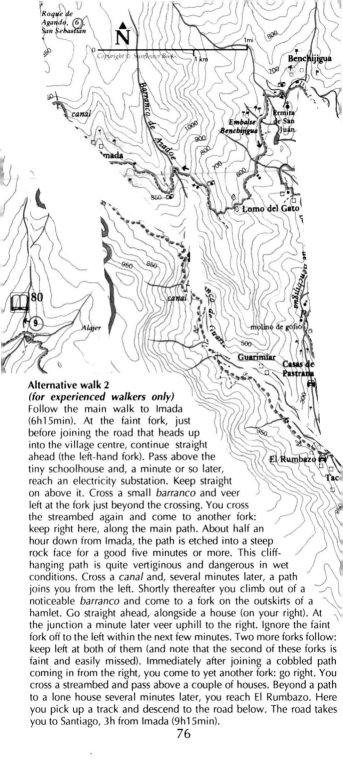

Alternative walk 2
(for experienced walkers only)

Follow the main walk to Imada
(6h15min). At the faint fork, just
before joining the road that heads up
into the village centre, continue straight
ahead (the left-hand fork). Pass above the
tiny schoolhouse and, a minute or so later,
reach an electricity substation. Keep straight
on above it. Cross a small *barranco* and veer
left at the fork just beyond the crossing. You cross
the streambed again and come to another fork:
keep right here, along the main path. About half an
hour down from Imada, the path is etched into a steep
rock face for a good five minutes or more. This cliff-
hanging path is quite vertiginous and dangerous in wet
conditions. Cross a *canal* and, several minutes later, a path
joins you from the left. Shortly thereafter you climb out of a
noticeable *barranco* and come to a fork on the outskirts of a
hamlet. Go straight ahead, alongside a house (on your right). At
the junction a minute later veer uphill to the right. Ignore the faint
fork off to the left within the next few minutes. Two more forks follow:
keep left at both of them (and note that the second of these forks is
faint and easily missed). Immediately after joining a cobbled path
coming in from the right, you come to yet another fork: go right. You
cross a streambed and pass above a couple of houses. Beyond a path
to a lone house several minutes later, you reach El Rumbazo. Here
you pick up a track and descend to the road below. The road takes
you to Santiago, 3h from Imada (9h15min).

76

bed, an enormous bulging pillar of rock high in the V of the *barranco* captures your attention — Roque de Agando (Walk 6). Cross the boulder-strewn streambed and follow it up the left-hand side (Picnic 8), passing a small *molino de gofio* — a mill where maize is ground and roasted*. Soon cross back to the right-hand side of the stream and aim for the large water tank not far ahead. The ravine gives one final twist, then straightens out to reveal Lomo del Gato, set on a terraced hillside adorned with palms. Grassy inclines and a loose scattering of pines make it reminiscent of an alpine scene.

The path flattens out as you head along the ravine walls. Keep right at a faint fork but, at the next fork (20 minutes later), veer left down towards Lomo del Gato. Head left again at the next fork; descend to the streambed, cross it, and climb the cobbled path opposite. On reaching the first house in Lomo del Gato, turn right to pass in front of it. Continue past a couple more houses, meet a fork and swing up left to a track (**2h 40min**). Some 20 minutes up the track, you pass below a great mass of rock bulging up out of the valley floor. A splendid (seasonal) cascade cuts down over it. A few minutes past here, just before a culvert, turn left on an overgrown goats' path and zigzag up into a small valley packed with mimosas. Soon you reach the remnants of an old cobbled path and a solitary dwelling on the crest of the ridge. Prickly pear surrounds you, but pines and eucalyptus begin appearing across the landscape. Pass the farmhouse and continue along the crest, ignoring

forks off to the right. Some 50m/yds beyond the house, come to a fork (just beyond a stone building): keep left and cross a dry streambed. Passing under loquat trees, keep straight ahead, below a cluttered yard, and in a few minutes reach a track and then a tiny roundabout (**4h20min**), near the Ermita de San Juán. You have a fine view over the hamlet of Benchijigua, with Roque de Agando (photograph page 74) standing guard in the background.

*Gofio is a popular local food. It's made into a thick paste and mixed with stews and soups or with honey, bananas, almonds, even cheese. The savouries are an acquired taste; the sweets are addictive! Freshly-ground *gofio* is very aromatic.

Follow the downhill track (behind a chained barrier). You spot a whole line of little houses above you, most of them uninhabited. Houseleeks and *verode* grow out of the roof tiles. A minute downhill, ignore a fork off to the left. Five minutes later, pass above a cluster of houses. When you are opposite the last house, turn right uphill on a path (the track descends at this point). In early spring the hillsides are splashed with pink almond blossoms. Catch a glimpse of the Benchijigua reservoir not far below. A path joins you from the right and you cross a crest to reach a farm. From here you will scale the steep escarpment ahead (near the narrow strip of almond trees on the left-hand side of it): follow the fence round the slope. You ascend to an overgrown almond orchard and then grassy inclines.

At about **5h**, just below some lichen-splattered walls, meet a faint T-junction and go right. Look back over the Benchijigua Valley, an immense bowl scooped out of the *cumbre*. Soon you cross over the pass and see a quite different landscape, where greenery is woven into the sheer valley walls. This valley drops down into another, deeper and darker. A derelict hamlet sits below, buried in prickly pear. You can glimpse Imada over a ridge that separates the two streambeds. Now head down to the right on the clear path. On crossing the streambed, immediately head right uphill. Several minutes later go left at a T-junction and round the Barranco de Guarimiar, a tributary of the Barranco de Santiago. The valley closes up into a shady passageway, dropping in leaps and bounds. Passing a lone house, descend into the terraced gardens of Imada, embellished with palms. Just over a smelly stream come to a fork: keep left to cross an even smellier stream. Reaching the houses (**6h15min**), turn up to the road. *(But note that those doing the Short walk or Alternative walk 2 should continue straight ahead here.)* A few minutes up the main road, come to a bar/shop, an ideal refuelling stop.

Your ongoing path begins by the streambed running alongside the shop. Keep straight uphill on this old stone-paved route, ignoring paths off right and left. Less than 20 minutes off the road, cross a small *canal,* and 45 minutes up cross over a pipe. The ascent ends some 30 minutes later — at last. Once on the crest, bear left and head straight over to the Alajeró road (**7h40min**). Turn right on this main road: the junction and your bus stop lie another 20 minutes uphill (**8h**).

9 ALAJERO • EL DRAGO • ERQUITO • ERQUE • ERQUE JUNCTION

Distance: 16.5km/10.2mi; 9h

Grade: very strenuous: overall ascent of 1100m/3600ft and descent of 800m/4775ft; **possibility of vertigo**

Equipment: walking boots, cardigan, anorak, long trousers, sunhat, rain-gear, picnic, plenty of water

How to get there: 🚌 to Alajeró (Timetable 21) or 🚌 to Playa de Santiago (Timetable 19) and taxi from there to Alajeró (13km)
To return: 🚌 from the Erque junction (Timetable 19)

In Erque's ravine

Short walks

1 Alajeró — *barranco* overlook — Alajeró (6.5km/4mi; 2h15min; easy-moderate descent and re-ascent of 200m/650ft; access/return by 🚌; stout shoes will suffice). Follow the main walk for 1h and return the same way.

2 Erque junction — Erque — Erque junction (up to 7.5km/4.7mi; 4h30min; moderate-strenuous descent/ascent of 450m/1475ft; equipment as above, but stout shoes will suffice). 🚌 or 🚌 (Timetable 19) to the Erque junction. Use the map to follow the tack and then the path to Erque. Return the same way (5km; 4h) or follow the track all the way back from Erque (7.5km/4h30min).

Everyone has ups and downs in life, but nowhere more so than on La Gomera. Getting anywhere involves a climb or a descent — often of hundreds of metres. This hike is no exception. Crossing the rock-littered, sunny south, you soak up the pastoral charm of lonely homesteads, roaming flocks and herds, and the distant jangling of bells. Declining plains, segmented by shady fathomless ravines, sit high above the sea. Inland the hills close in on each other, leaving only breathing space for the two isolated villages of Erque and Erquito.

The interesting church of Alajeró is your **starting point**. With your back to it (facing the cemetery), take the steps leading off the square (50m/yds off to your right). Straight away join a track, keeping left. Out of the village, you pass the last of the palms and head across fields. La Fortaleza (cover photograph) is the large, flat-topped mound of rock you can see through a gap in the hills ahead (Picnic 9a).

The first, and most charming, of the homesteads en route is Magaña; it soon appears on the ridge opposite, set in an apron of prickly pear. When the track ends, overlooking a ravine, continue straight ahead, following the path dipping down into the *barranco*. A treacle-coloured reservoir sits in the valley floor below. Just above the reservoir your way forks: veer right and circle the reservoir to cross the *barranco*. Climbing out, head up tabaiba-covered slopes, where the occasional small bush of *lingua de gato* (cat's tongue), a shiny green, sticky-leafed plant is seen. Under 10 minutes up pass a fork off right to Magaña and a minute later come to the

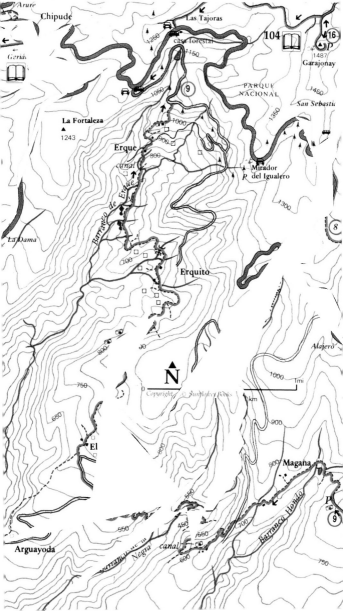

crest. Look back to the hamlet: a lovely house with balconies sits embedded in rock, accompanied by other smaller buildings.

Continuing along the ridge, you circle a more modest homestead and cross over a small streambed. Above the streambed come onto a road and turn left. When the road ends 15 minutes later, find the continuation of your path off to the right, over rocky terrain: it's a faint path that cuts straight round the hillside. In a few minutes some abandoned houses suddenly come to light. Your way skirts to the right of them. Then, without warning, you're overlooking an enormously deep ravine (**1h**). *Short walk 1 turns back from here.*

A tiny group of cottages fastened high up on the ravine walls opposite catches your eye. The route will head straight up through this derelict hamlet (La Manteca); what a view you'll have! Descending further, faded splashes of red paint soon alert you to your turn-off down into the *barranco.* An animal trail brings you to the main path in about five minutes. More plots begin to appear — on narrow shelves in the wall, on top of rocky outcrops, along the streambed. Most lie abandoned. When you meet a fork a few minutes along, bear left. At **1h30min** you cross a trickling stream. Some good-sized pools lie above you. Heading left, you pick up the remains of a cobbled path climbing the hillside and cross another streambed on rose-coloured rock. Then round a corner and take the faint fork to the right; the first of the strength-sapping ascents is about to begin. At about **2h10min** you're looking up into La Manteca, which appears to reflect the way you yourself may be feeling: it's in a state of collapse! An odd mixture of buildings lies before you — some are just faces in the hillside. Twisting up between the houses, you soon mount a plain and head through some fields, where cereals are grown in summer months. Arguayoda reveals another corner of itself, cosily sited on the edge

of the plain — a pleasant piece of decor when seen from here. (Arguayoda is one of those villages that loses its charm when you approach; the main walk doesn't visit it.)

On reaching a track (where a left turn leads to Arguayoda), turn right for El Drago, the dark scattering of houses up ahead. When you reach them, leave the track on the first sharp bend: fork off left and follow the path up through the hamlet (**3h30min**). In the clump of decaying houses, ignore the white arrows everywhere and, past the houses, swing up left. When you come to the last buildings, turn off to the right. A steady climb follows, and La Fortaleza re-appears.

You come to a track which joins another, some metres along to the right. Follow the track to the left. Some 20 minutes later, round a bend to find the hillside plummeting away below into a vast deep valley — a magnificent sight. Your route is now a ledge cut out of the face of the hill. The track comes to a dead end, and you follow the path leading off it, downhill to the left, descending into a thin grove of almond trees (not far beyond a path coming in from the right). Not long after, pass through a cluster of deserted cottages. Just before crossing the *barranco*, the way forks: head right. Refill your canteens at the spring here; the next gruelling ascent is just round the corner. Several minutes from the spring, pass a fork off to the left and come to abandoned Erquito. (At this point, if you don't think you can stand any more ups and downs, scramble straight down the hillside, zigzagging through the terracing to the dirt road; then follow it left to the main road. This doesn't save any time, but is easier on the legs.)

Your faint path heads past the abandoned shop and a shed. In a few minutes (just beyond a streambed crossing), a small footbridge takes you over a deep *barranco*. Scaling a steep rocky ridge (unnerving for vertigo sufferers), you initially follow a telephone cable. Ignore the faint branch-off right some 20 minutes up; keep left round the crest. A few of Erque's houses appear, below towering ravine walls. A stream flows down the valley floor, and small waterfalls tumble down the terraces. Ignore a faint fork off to the left nearer the streambed. Cross and re-cross a tiny watercourse and then head over the overgrown streambed. Your route (now very faint) runs up the right-hand side of the terracing. In a few minutes, pass to the right of a house and continue straight uphill over bare rock, crossing a narrow irrigation channel. Ignore all paths off to the right. You swing up to a track in Erque (**6h30min**).

A few minutes along the track, turn right to rejoin the path as it cuts up the hillside (just before the first house on the left). Further up the ridge, a couple of stone buildings serve as landmarks. When you meet the track again head left to the main road and bus stop (**9h**).

10 CHIPUDE • GERIAN • VALLE GRAN REY

Distance: 9.5km/5.9mi; under 3h

Grade: easy-moderate descent of 800m/2600ft

Equipment: stout shoes, cardigan, anorak, long trousers, sunhat, raingear, picnic, water

How to get there: 🚌 to Chipude (Timetable 19)
To return: 🚌 from Valle Gran Rey (Timetable 19)

Short walks

1 Chipude — Gerián — Chipude (10km/6.2mi; 3h; easy descent/ascent of 350m/1150ft; access/equipment as above). Follow the main walk to Gerián and return the same way for the bus (Timetable 19).

2 Los Descansaderos — Ermita de los Reyes — Valle Gran Rey (4km/2.5mi; 1h; easy descent of 400m/1300ft; wear stout shoes). Valle Gran Rey 🚌 to Los Descansaderos (Timetable 19). Use the map on pages 84-85 to descend to the *ermita* via the *barranco* (red circles indicate a short-cut path just after you cross the *barranco*), then go on to the main road for the return bus (opposite the Centro Cultural).

Alternative walk: Chipude — Los Granados (5km/3mi; 1h45min; steep, **vertiginous and potentially dangerous** descent of 700m/2300ft; access/return, equiment as above). ***Recommended for experienced walkers only, and only in dry weather.*** Description pages 84-85.

This fairly easy walk makes a 'grand entrance' into the Valley of the Great King — Valle Gran Rey. Leaving Chipude, the highest village on the island (1050m/3450ft), you may well set off in a playful mist; it creeps down on you, then disperses in wisps, revealing picture-postcard views. Strolling down rambling plains, unaware of the great gulches that plummet away on either side, your attention is drawn to line upon line of crumbled stone walls. Amidst these walls, on the edge of a sheer ravine, sits the hamlet of Gerián. Gerián's *barranco*, the first you cross, is but a baby compared to the one that follows, the Valle Gran Rey.

Setting out from the church in Chipude, follow the road towards San Sebastián. At the La Dama junction, turn right downhill on an earthen track, skirting the central plateau. Vineyards fill the basin below. La Fortaleza (cover photograph) is the solid crown of basalt dominating the landscape. On cloudless days, you seem to be walking straight towards El Hierro. La Palma rises out of the sea on the right like two companion whales.

Farmstead met about halfway along the track to Gerián

Mists keep the inclines fresh and green with a thin carpet of grass, but the trees have long since vanished. Your route meanders lazily down the crest. Ignore the forks to the left. Shortly you're looking across a razor-sharp ridge towards the heights of the Gran Rey ravine. Here's where the mists will put on a show for you.

Gerián is in sight **45min** into the walk, and at about **1h** you're standing above it. Follow the path downhill for a couple of minutes, perhaps to sit on the ledge and drink in the lonely beauty. Then return to the corner of the track and follow the continuation of your path up to the left. Soon a tiny chapel appears. Head for it on a well-worn path, passing through a gap in the wall. The views from the chapel (*ermita*) are fine, and you can see your ongoing route crossing the valley wall opposite.

Drop down off this balcony to continue round the hillside. In a minute the way forks; keep downhill and briefly walk alongside (or in) a watercourse. Cross the watercourse and descend to the valley floor, cross the streambed (**1h30min**), and then swing back left. When you meet a fork in a few minutes, keep left. Ascending to a pass, you look down into emerald-green pools in the *barranco* bed.

Cross the top of the crest at **1h45min**, keeping right. Go straight on over the ridge and down into Valle Gran

Alternative walk
From Chipude's church, cross the road to the Bar La Candelaria. Follow the cobbled path at the right of it and continue to the road: turn left. 50m/yds uphill, go right on a track. At a fork, go right. The track ends: go right towards a house, but bear left at once. At a junction,

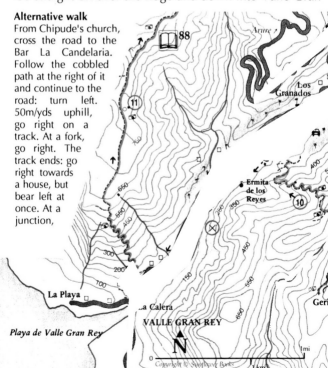

Rey. An impressive view greets you straight away, and more views unravel as you descend. You look across severe, charred-brown ravine walls that seal off the valley. The Los Reyes chapel rests at the mouth of the ravine. The downhill path is now steep and gravelly, so descend with care. The enormity of the valley is evident minutes later, when you peer down onto the Aguada area, where a mosaic of vivid green plots stretches across the floor. Palms abound, and the bright-white dwellings only serve to enhance the greenery. Fifteen minutes down you pass a goats' pen. Milking begins at about midday: if you have time, watch the goatherd work his old alsatian — it's a marvellous dog.

The path twirls steeply down, and the rest of the valley opens up. Curling up and over a rocky ridge, you come to a fork: go straight down (to the right). Half a minute later, keep left (where a path veers off right). At **2h25min** cross the streambed. Just beyond it, you pass the first houses — two charming cottages with colourful gardens. Head left at the junction below them, making for the chapel. Just across the chapel yard, descend steps on the right. Cross the *barranco* floor and climb to the road. Follow the road downhill to the left. The bus stop sits just above the telephone box and taxi stand, up to your right, opposite the Centro Cultural (under **3h**).

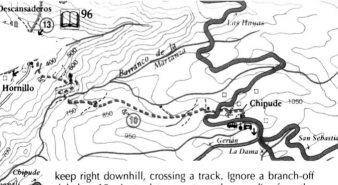

keep right downhill, crossing a track. Ignore a branch-off right but, 15 minutes later, meet a path ascending from the right: go right, then fork left down an old cobbled path (obscured by grass). Over the streambed, climb left uphill, to a pass. Head right from here, and clamber over a rock-slide. Descend a vertiginous, precipitous cleft, then fork right down a path (small cairn). A path joins from the right: follow it left, and keep left down to the road. Turn left on the road for 50m/yds, then go right on a path and left at the first fork. When you reach the road again follow it to the main road. The bus stop is just downhill to the left.

11 VALLE GRAN REY • ARURE • CHORROS DE EPINA

Map begins on page 84   **Distance:** 14km/8.7mi; 7h45min

Grade: very strenuous, with overall ascents of over 1100m/3600ft and a steep (**sometimes vertiginous**) descent of 300m/1000ft. A path at the end of the hike is overgrown and may have to be avoided, **adding another hour to the walk** (see footnote page 89). *Can be very cold!*

Equipment: stout shoes or walking boots, cardigan, anorak, long trousers, long-sleeved shirt, stick to beat back blackberry bushes, sunhat, raingear, picnic, plenty of water

How to get there: 🚌 to Valle Gran Rey, 'La Calera' (Timetable 19)
To return: taxi from the restaurant at Chorros de Epina (see * page 89) either to Arure or Valle Gran Rey, for the return bus (Timetable 19)

Short walks: for both, take the Valle Gran Rey 🚌 to the Arure junction and start at the Mirador del Santo; equipment as above.

1 Arure — Valle Gran Rey (7.5km/4.7mi; 3h; moderate: a steep zig-zagging descent of 800m/2600ft on a stony path). See map on page 88 to start; continue with the map on page 84. This is the start of the main walk, in reverse. Return 🚌 from Valle Gran Rey (Timetable 19)

2 Arure — Chorros de Epina (6.5km/4mi; 3h05min; moderate descent/ascent of 300m/1000ft). Follow the main walk from the 4h40min-point; map page 88. Return as main walk.

Alternative walks (access/grade as main walk for both, plus *additional* descents of 600m/1950ft on steep slippery paths)

1 Valle Gran Rey — Chorros de Epina — Camino Forestal de la Meseta — Vallehermoso (20.5km/12.7mi; 10h45mi). Follow the main walk to Chorros de Epina, then use the notes on page 88. Note: the path to Vallehermoso is narrow, slippery when wet, and might prove vertiginous for some; it is also becoming quite overgrown. Return by 🚌 from Vallehermoso (Timetable 20).

2 Valle Gran Rey — Chorros de Epina — Santa Clara — Valle-hermoso (22.5km/14mi; 10h45min). Follow the main walk to Chorros de Epina, then refer to the map and notes on page 89. Return by 🚌 from Vallehermoso (Timetable 20).

If you're a masochist and like to start the day with the thought that it couldn't get any worse/tougher, then this is the walk for you! Most people will find the two Short walks, each covering half of the route, more enjoyable. Leaving Valle Gran Rey, you scale the preci-pitous rock walls that overshadow La Calera (the village centre) and head for the north. From the summits, your view dips into every nook and cranny of the Gran Rey ravine and out over the desolate southwest. Botanists will relish the plant life by the cliffs at Chorros de Epina.

The most confusing part of this walk is **starting out** from La Calera. Your ascent begins just downhill from the bus stop. Climb the alley between the Parada Bar and the Ayuntamiento (town hall). Take the first right turn and continue uphill between the rest of the houses. Paths join you all the way: when in doubt, keep *uphill*, rather than branching off. (Small yellow crosses mark the initial flight of steps.) In just over **10min** reach a lookout balcony. Take the clear narrow path at the rear of this viewing platform; it curves round the hillside back into the *barranco*. Within a few minutes you come onto the beginning of the old path. A stone wall follows it uphill a short way, so it's easily spotted, but you'll have to scramble up to it. As you climb, banana plantations, a deep blue sea, and dark bluffs come into view — followed by a glimpse of Aguada, a shrill patch of greenery in its monochrome surroundings. El Hierro is the island you can see (more than likely under cloud).

A solid slog lasting well over an hour brings you to a lateral ridge, from where you look straight down onto La Playa and Valle Gran Rey, the setting dramatised by the jagged ridges tumbling down alongside you. At about **2h15min** you reach the crest, where goats graze the remains of terracing. Continue up the crest, to catch sight of Arure, set back in a shallow gulley on the edge of the plateau. A few minutes later, pass to the left of a sunken tank and an igloo-shaped rock construction. The country villages of Chipude, El Cercado and Las Hayas (from right to left) soon come into view, settings for Walks 10 and 13. Pass the fork off left to the triangulation point at the summit (**3h05min**).

Crossing over a ridge, you briefly catch a view of the southwest and overlook a formidable landscape of bare rock, devoid of life and drained of colour. La Palma lies before you above a cape of lingering cloud. Come upon a track at **3h30min** and continue along it, keeping right at the intersection a few minutes later. You may pass beehives along the track here, so go quietly. Less than

An unfinished house sits among asphodels en route to Arure.

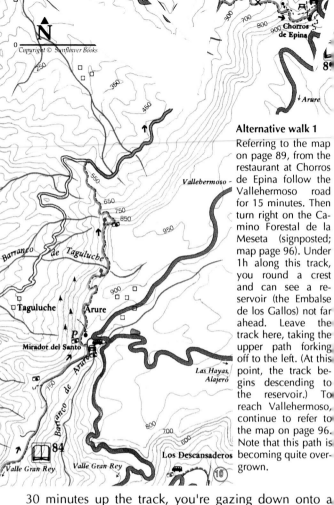

Referring to the map on page 89, from the restaurant at Chorros de Epina follow the Vallehermoso road for 15 minutes. Then turn right on the Camino Forestal de la Meseta (signposted; map page 96). Under 1h along this track, you round a crest and can see a reservoir (the Embalse de los Gallos) not far ahead. Leave the track here, taking the upper path forking off to the left. (At this point, the track begins descending to the reservoir.) To reach Vallehermoso, continue to refer to the map on page 96. Note that this path is becoming quite overgrown.

30 minutes up the track, you're gazing down onto a patchwork of gardens in a tremendously deep basin, and soon Taguluche is seen. Crossing over the ridge for the umpteenth time, you descend to a car-park, just beyond which you turn off left on a cobbled path to the Mirador del Santo, overlooking the Tagaluche ravine, and the San Juán chapel (**4h40min**; Picnic 11; *Short walks 11-1 and 11-2 begin here*).

Take the path behind the chapel, keeping right at the fork a minute along. Brushing through a light scattering of pines, you edge along the escarpment. The views are stupendous, but you may find this part of the walk unnerving. A very steep descent (initially on a stone-paved path) follows, and some 20 minutes from the *mirador* you strike a section of path that is extremely vertiginous. You're now following a goats' path below vertical rock walls. At about **5h20min** you're standing at the edge of a vast basin, looking down on the large farming settlement of Alojera — an unexpected sight in this bleak landscape. The heights, benefitting from the trade winds, are noticeably greener than the declining hills, some of them totally bare. A slippery, gravelly descent drops you down over the ridge to the road

Turn right on the road (**5h40min**), walking in the shadows of the *cumbre*. Alojera is constantly in view below. A relaxing stroll lies ahead of you now. Some 25 minutes along the road, the sound of gushing water announces a spring. Meet the Alojera road (**6h30min**) and turn right. Not far uphill (just before passing under a telephone cable), turn right on a stony path climbing the hillside (keep right at a fork met almost at once and left at the next fork). A wide cobbled path, sometimes vanishing under lush grass, takes you up through pastureland. A faint trail takes you up and over the last of the grassy hills. The Restaurante Los Chorros de

Epina comes into sight, set on the edge of the *cumbre.* Pass to the right of a sunken water tank, cut across the hillside to a clear path, and bear right. Keep right again at a fork*; at **7h45min** come to a chapel and a lovely shady picnic site. The bar/restaurant, where you may be lucky enough to find a taxi, is just beyond here.

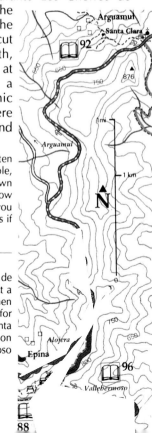

*The path just before the chapel is often overgrown. Should it become impassable, you will have to scramble and slide down the hillside to the road below and follow the road out to Epina, which will cost you about another hour. Please allow for this if you are catching a bus or being met.

Alternative walk 2

Downhill from the restaurant at Chorros de Epina, turn left for Alojera/Taguluche. At a junction, keep right for Arguamul. Then fork right on the first track you come to for Chigere/Santa Clara. Follow it to the Santa Clara chapel. From there, use the map on page 92 to continue on to Vallehermoso (Walk 12 in reverse).

12 VALLEHERMOSO • CHIGERE • PLAYA DE VALLEHERMOSO • VALLEHERMOSO

Distance: 14.5km/9mi; 6h30min

Grade: strenuous; overall ascent of 750m/2450ft and descent of 800m/2600ft. The descent to Playa de Vallehermoso is very steep, gravelly, and **vertiginous;** *only recommended for very experienced walkers.*

Equipment: stout shoes or walking boots, sunhat, cardigan, anorak, long trousers, raingear, picnic, water; additionally, swimwear in the summer, when the pool is filled — the sea is far too dangerous!

How to get there and return: 🚌 or 🚐 (Timetable 20) to/from Vallehermoso

Alternative walks

1 Vallehermoso — Santa Clara — Vallehermoso (10km/6.2mi; 5h; strenuous ascent/descent of 550m/1800ft). 🚌 or 🚐 (Timetable 20) to/from Vallehermoso. Follow the main walk to the Santa Clara chapel (3h) and return same way.

2 Vallehermoso — Santa Clara — Chorros de Epina (11.5km/7.1mi; 5h; strenuous ascent of 550m/1800ft at the start — the rest is a doddle!) 🚐 to Vallehermoso (Timetable 20). Follow the main walk to the Santa Clara chapel (3h), then turn left on the track (the main walk bears right to Chigere). Now refer to the map on page 89. When you meet the track coming in from Arguamul, keep left. At the Alojera junction keep left again, crossing over the *cumbre.* At the main Vallehermoso road turn right for Chorros de Epina. *Note:* from Chorros de Epina, you could use the maps on pages 88 and then 84, to continue to Valle Gran Rey via Arure (Walk 11 in reverse).

Reaching Vallehermoso is an expedition in itself. Your bus crawls over a mountainous relief carved up by plunging ravines, which leave a skeleton of fine-lined ridges tapering off into the sea. Each new view is better than the last one. The walk gives you commanding panoramas of the normally inaccessible north coast and beyond — on clear days — to Tenerife and her showpiece El Teide. The solitude of the pastoral outpost of Chigere, abandoned a couple of decades ago, makes an ideal lunch-stop before the exhilarating descent to the beach. This descent really does take your breath away!

From Vallehermoso's village square/bus stop **start out** by heading up the narrow street at the right of the Bar Central. Pass above the church, meet the Valle Gran Rey road, and follow it left uphill as far as the first bend. Here take the first turn-off right, to the cemetery. Continue from the cemetery on a path: descend into the *barranco* floor, where you cross a footbridge and climb to a couple of houses opposite. Red dots and circles lie at frequent intervals. Roque Cano (photograph page 101), an enormous spearhead of rock overshadowing the village, commands your attention.

Just before you begin the steep descent to the beach at Vallehermoso, continue on the track for this superb view of the north coast. Then begin the descent: if you can handle the first few minutes, the rest will pose no problems. Make for the lateral ridge that slides off into the valley below (even though you can hardly believe that this is your route down!). The beach is the most dangerous on the island; to swim here would be madness — the pool speaks for itself. But the setting is dramatic: old buildings, perched on seashore salients, speak of a once-flourishing port.

Just below the houses, come to a fork: head left, and steps take you up against the houses, before you curve round to head up into the Barranco de la Era Nueva. *Sabina* — an indigenous juniper — is abundant here. Continue straight on some six minutes up from the houses (where a path forks off to plots below). Go right at the next fork (five minutes later), and right again at the next fork (half a minute beyond and above a large water tank). Soon you begin a series of streambed crossings, and the real ascent begins. Leave behind the cane, *tabaiba,* brambles, ferns and aromatic *artemisia* for the evergreen forest. Falcons hover overhead.

After crossing the streambed for the last time, you pass a faint fork to the left. Scaling a ridge, your view expands to encompass the central spine of the island, curling around this immense depression of valleys. A cape of dark cloud, pierced by the occasional ray of sunlight, rests on the *cumbre.* Entering heather, the way flattens out. A scattering of white houses in the distance reveals Tamagarda. The path edges its way along the top of the ravine, close to the tree-line, until you reach a flat crest. If the mist hasn't enveloped you, you'll see the Ermita de Santa Clara over to the right (**3h**). An earthen track runs across in front of you. If the mist lifts, you have splendid views over the remote village of Arguamul and the group of peaked rocks off its shore.

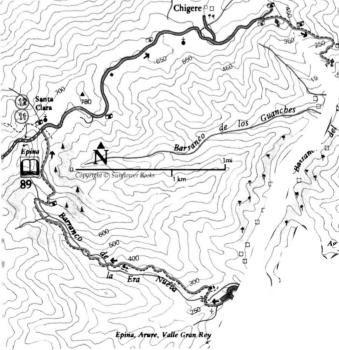

Epina, Arure, Valle Gran Rey

To continue to Chigere, turn right and follow the track past the chapel. *(Alternative walk 2 bears left here for Epina; Alternative walk 1 turns back to Vallehermoso.)* Startled partridges may dart out of bushes as you pass, screeching blue murder. Ten minutes from the chapel, ignore a track off to the right. At about **3h25min** another chapel comes into sight, laid bare to the winds on an open crest. Passing it, you descend into a high valley. A rainbow of pastel pinks, browns, greys, mauves and yellows glows out of a bare hillside below. Soon a few stray palms adorning a rocky ridge disclose Chigere's whereabouts. This decayed settlement of stone houses with tiled rooftops sits almost unnoticed against the rocks. Turn off left for the hamlet. You over-look a hillside wooded in young pines. Another fine vista stretches before you: streams of valleys pouring out of a landscape of ever-dividing ridges. In Chigere (**3h40min**) you'll find sunshine: soak it up!

Then rejoin the main track and continue downhill. Before long, you catch sight of the coast, and a stunning seascape unravels. Ridges, serrating the coastline, tumble off into a faintly green sea. Vallehermoso comes out of hiding. A valley lined with banana groves trails down from it. The entire countryside is freckled with *sabina.* It is at this viewpoint that you turn off right for the beach: a small pile of rocks indicates your zig-zagging goats' trail. (Before setting off, continue along the track for another 100m/yds, to the hillock in front of you, to capture the views shown on pages 90-91). Then begin the descent. After two minutes, the worst is be-hind you. *Always* keep your eyes on the path, although the views are irresistible! Your view soon stretches all the way up the Barranco del Valle. Some 25 minutes down, the way swings right to cross a steep slope and join a streambed — another unnerving bit of path. Heading down the streambed, watch out for broken glass among the rocks and stones. Ignore a path joining from the left; pass below a house and take the path to the right. Reach the road a few minutes later. Now the beach is just downhill (**5h**).

Return to Vallehermoso by following the road south uphill — a gentle ascent. As the afternoon shadows creep across the ravine walls, you amble alongside a valley floor crammed with banana groves and cane. A stream bubbles away below you. Beyond a new botani-cal garden, come into Vallehermoso at **6h30min**.

13 VALLEHERMOSO • LA MESETA • JARDIN DE LAS CRECES • LAS HAYAS • VALLE GRAN REY

NB: This walk is in two parts; see IMPORTANT NOTE on page 96

Distance: 16km/10mi; 6h45min

Grade: strenuous, with an ascent of 600m/1950ft to start (**possibility of vertigo**) and a very steep, sometimes stony, descent of 750m/2450ft at the end. The path up to La Meseta is becoming overgrown.

Equipment: stout shoes or walking boots, sunhat, cardigan, anorak, long trousers, long-sleeved shirt, stick for beating back blackberry thorns, raingear, water, picnic (or have lunch at Las Hayas).

How to get there: 🚌 to Vallehermoso (Timetable 20)

To return: 🚌 from Valle Gran Rey, Los Granados (Timetable 19)

Short walk: Las Hayas — Valle Gran Rey, Los Granados (4.5km/2.8mi; 1h50min; moderate, with a very steep, sometimes stony, descent of 750m/2450ft). 🚌 to Las Hayas (Timetable 19) and return as main walk. Follow the main walk from the 5h-point.

I'm not quite sure what I most look forward to on this walk — the dramatic introduction to Valle Gran Rey ... or Doña Efigenia's meals at Las Hayas. 'La Montaña' is no fancy restaurant with an à la carte menu; there is no menu. Just eat what's put in front of you; you'll be glad you did. As for the trek, it gives you an excellent cross-section of the island's landscapes, from the peaceful countryside of Vallehermoso to the tourist enclaves of Valle Gran Rey. And in between, a snippet of the island's most prized treasure — the laurel forest.

Set out by leaving Vallehermoso on the road branching left off the square, past the Banco de Santander. Heading up into the Barranco del Ingenio you wind above banana plots and vegetable gardens. Twenty

The forestry road at La Meseta, met after three hours' walking

minutes up the road, turn right on a track that cuts up into a narrow *barranco* (the first track you reach, just where the road curves sharp left). A stream runs below on your right. You will follow this track for the next hour or so. Note a fork off left and, later, a fork off right, beyond which the track flattens out and crosses the crest. Here you pick up your path to La Meseta: your path is at the right, on the bend in the track; it continues up the ridge. (Or pick up your path a little further on, directly opposite a water tank. If you take this path, veer right immediately to mount the crest and join the main path; don't continue left round the hillside.)

The route is very straightforward from here to La Meseta — remain on or near the crest all the way up. It's a steep climb. Roque Cano (photograph page 101) is the monstrous rock that disrupts the landscape behind you. A corner of Vallehermoso comes into view, with its *barranco* and, on the other side of the ridge, you look down onto small clusters of homesteads in the Barranco del Ingenio. Nearing La Meseta, a bit of narrow path, along a steep overgrown hillside, forces you to walk *very slowly and carefully* (especially in wet weather) and some people might find this stretch unnerving.

At **3h** you meet the track shown opposite — the La Meseta forestry road *(camino forestal)*. Turn right: an easy hour's stroll to the main road is now ahead of you. The track skirts the edge of the forest, and you can see the enchanting village of Macayo set high on a ridge amidst palms. Hopefully you have transport waiting for you on the main road (**4h**); if not, continue along this road (see 'IMPORTANT NOTE' on page 96).

***

Rejoining the walk at the Camino Forestal Jardín de las Creces (experimental forestry station), you head off into the laurel forest. Tall trees padded in moss grow around you, and the air is damp and crisp. Beyond the pretty *zona recreativa* your way continues to the right, behind the barrier. As you near the edge of the wood, the trees thin out and more light penetrates. Soft spongy grass covers the floor. Giant heath trees first appear in small numbers and then form a wood of their own — some growing to a height of 15m/50ft. When you come to a fork, keep right downhill towards a fence. The track fizzles out: follow the path leading off it. You leave the heather for fields lightly sprinkled with palms. Keep left at both forks you encounter when passing through the

IMPORTANT NOTE

In a highly-commendable attempt to protect the laurel forest, ICONA has closed off all footpaths except for its own waymarked nature trails. To police further paths would be impossible. Please obey the signs! To comply with these regulations, I have split this walk into two halves. Arrange to be met at the entrance to the Camino Forestal de la Meseta and taken on to Jardín de las Creces, or walk there along the road (some 6.5km). If you walk along the road, use the map on page 89 to locate a short cut below Chorros de Epina; it cuts out a bend in the road.

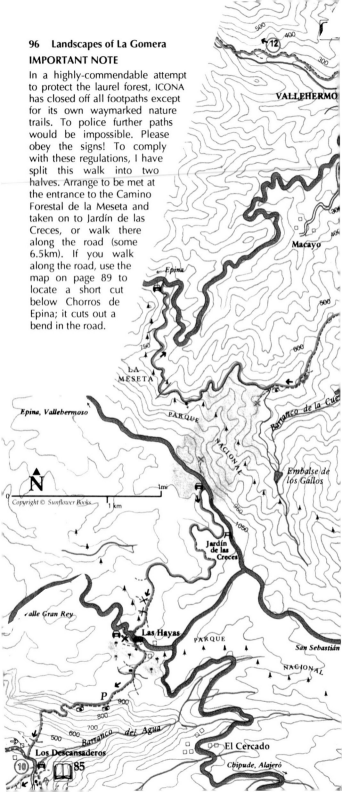

VALLEHERMO

Macayo

Epina

LA MESETA

Epina, Vallehermoso

PARQUE

Barranco de la Cue

NACIONAL

Embalse de los Gallos

N

Copyright © Sunflower Books

1mi

1 km

Jardín de las Creces

Valle Gran Rey

Las Hayas

PARQUE

San Sebastián

NACIONAL

P

Barranco del Agua

Los Descansaderos

El Cercado

85

Chipude, Alajeró

vineyards and garden plots. A few houses hidden in trees and bushes ahead announce Las Hayas ... and Doña Efigenia. Look over your shoulder now: you'll see clouds roll down over the trees and then suddenly rise and vanish. Reach the Valle Gran Rey road and go left downhill to La Montaña (**5h**). *Buen provecho! But note:* eating here *takes time.* Make sure you don't have to rush for a bus! (Picnickers: 20 minutes ahead is an unsurpassed setting for *your* lunch break.)

Leave the road a minute above the restaurant: go right on an earthen path, opposite a driveway. Brush against a house and head down into a combe of palms. Some 50m/yds along, the path bears right, down towards a house. Just before you reach it, another path cuts in front of you: keep left downhill, along a splendid 'avenue' of palms. Cross a dry streambed and continue on the main path, overlooking grassy plots and a mass of palms. A short climb takes you over a low crest. Pass a dwelling and cross straight over a track, to descend into another valley of palms. Meet a fork and head right. Then cross another low crest and overlook an abyss — the Barranco del Agua, a tributary of the Gran Rey. La Fortaleza, the table-topped rock shown on the cover, sits in the background. Soon the striking grandeur of the Valle Gran Rey, a luxuriant tapestry of banana groves, cane and vegetable gardens, becomes apparent (Picnic 13), but *don't* go too near the precipice!

Coming onto cobbles, you now begin a *very steep* descent down a zigzagging path; it's a fine piece of workmanship, and not at all vertiginous. Cross a small watercourse and keep left at a fork just beyond it, to step down to a road in Los Descansaderos (**6h20min**). Referring to the map on page 84, turn left down the palm-flooded valley floor. Some five minutes along, go right on a paved path (if you miss it, you'll come to a roadside water tank some 40m/yds further on). Straight into the path, fork left, as the red circles indicate. At the next fork keep right. Just before reaching the road again, you pass straight over an intersection (well marked with the red circles). The road takes you to the Valle Gran Rey road at Los Granados, where the bus stop is a minute downhill to the left (**6h45min**).

14 AGULO • GARAJONAY NATIONAL PARK VISITORS' CENTRE • EMBALSE DE AMALA-HUIGUE • EL TION • VALLEHERMOSO

NB: The Visitors' Centre is open 09.30-16.30 Tuesdays to Saturdays

Distance: 14km/8.7mi; 7h

Grade: fairly strenuous, with overall ascent/descent of 700m/2300ft; beyond El Tión, the descent is steep, on a gravelly path (**possibility of vertigo**); some paths are overgrown.

Equipment: stout shoes or walking boots, sunhat, cardigan, anorak, long trousers, long-sleeved shirt, stick for beating back blackberry thorns, raingear, picnic, water

How to get there: 🚌 to Agulo (Timetable 20)
To return: 🚌 from Vallehermoso (Timetable 20)

Short walks

1 Agulo — Embalse de Amalahuigue — Las Rosas (7.5km/4.7mi; 4h15min; fairly strenuous, with overall ascent of 700m/2300ft; access as above). Follow the main walk to the 4h-point, then cross the road, head straight down a narrow tarred lane into Las Rosas, and continue on to the main road. The bus stop (Vallehermoso 🚌, Timetable 20) is down to the right, at the signposted turn-off to La Palmita.

2 Vallehermoso — Embalse de Amalahuigue — Las Rosas (7km/4.3mi; 3h45min; fairly strenuous ascent of 550m/1800ft, some of it on a steep, gravelly path). Follow the map on page 92, and then the map below; this is the end of the walk, but in reverse. Cross the wall of the Amalahuigue Reservoir, then continue as Short walk 1 above.

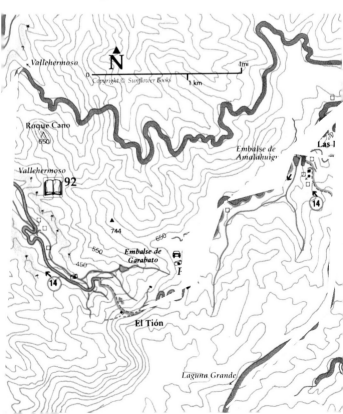

You'll remember this walk for the enchanting valleys. The first one you encounter, finely etched into the landscape, leaves a deep impression — both figuratively and literally. You climb into scrub-smeared hills, dotted with dwellings. Approaching the tree-line, settlement subsides, and from the top of a crest you overlook an immense cauldron of cascading ridges. Vallehermoso sits in their midst. A most rewarding descent follows, as you drop into a plunging valley drenched with palms, its high rock walls flecked with pines. Here the terraced plots are a work of art; you have the feeling you could stroll in this valley forever.

Off the bus, **start off** by heading up the road towards Vallehermoso, and take the first right turn. Follow this cobbled street straight through Agulo to the village square with its strange domed church and old houses with high, latticed windows. Banana groves sever the three separate *barrios* that make up the village. Some 25m/yds beyond the cemetery, climb a wide path up the hillside. Tenerife sits just across the sea, a vista of which Agulo is very proud (Picnic 15). Reaching the Vallehermoso road again, find your continuing path just

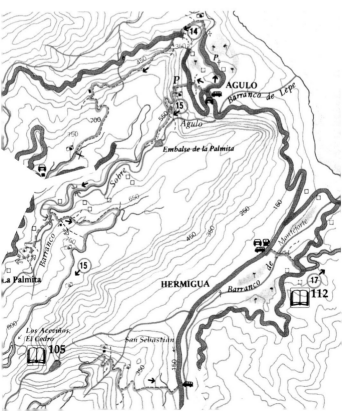

uphill on the left: head steeply uphill on cobbles (ignore the faint branch-off to the left). Faded paint dots mark the route. (Keep left at a faint fork.) Just beyond a charming old abandoned house (about an hour off the road), your path swings abruptly up to the left: don't continue straight ahead! You reach the crest of the ridge, where the path fades on the clay surface: head right, in or alongside a deeply-eroded watercourse. You cross a ridge soaked in rich volcanic hues. On meeting a track, head right uphill. A sweeping view up the ravine follows. Joining a road, you come to the Visitors' Centre (**3h15min**). Take a break and watch the informative film devoted to the Garajonay National Park.

Revived, set off up the adjoining Laguna Grande road. Beyond the La Palmita/El Cedro turn-off, turn down an earthen track (the second one you come to) for the Amalahuigue Reservoir. (There is sometimes a chain across the entrance to this track.) Almost at once the track forks: bear left; then, just beyond another barrier (this one unchained), fork right downhill on a path. Metres/yards along, a power pole bearing two red circles confirms the route. Cross a streambed and head straight up the other side, pass between a couple of houses, and climb a semi-clad ridge. On reaching the last houses, on the top of the crest, you brush alongside the house furthest right. Then swing down to the right, to rejoin the overgrown path rounding the hillside. Here you're on the edge of the heather belt bordering the laurel forest. A few minutes past the last house you come out on a crest and pass above two power pylons. Continue left round the hillside and in a minute or two come to another pylon on the next crest. Drop down over the crest. A path cuts in front of you: follow it to the right. A steep descent (keep straight on, ignoring branch-offs) takes you down beside water pipes. Pass two water tanks and soon come onto a track. A little further on, just past an unfinished house, take a path and steps descending the left side of the crest. Then step down to a road and the Amalahuigue Reservoir (**4h**). *(The Short walks head down to Las Rosas here.)*

Crossing the reservoir wall, you look down into Las Rosas. At the end of the wall, bear left on the road. As you circle the top of the valley, two tracks join from the right and, immediately after, you have a good view of Roque Cano (see opposite), a landmark for all walks around Vallehermoso. When the tar ends, continue on gravel. You look across an immense cauldron filled with cascading ridges. Bright green vegetable plots glow in their surroundings (Picnic 14). Passing two forks to the left, bear right and descend into the valley. Hugging the sheer hillside, the track winds down to El Tión, a couple of solitary homesteads. Then, just beyond a fork to the right, the track ends. Take the path descending to the right. You drop down to terraces and cut across them to some stone houses balancing on a ridge high above Vallehermoso, a perfect picnic spot. The onward route is straight down this sheer-sided ridge, and inexperienced walkers may find the first few minutes unnerving. This gravelly path drops you onto a track: descend into the valley shown below, the highlight of the walk. Follow the track to the main road (see map on page 92). The bus stop is in the square, to your left (**7h**).

Roque Cano rises above the 'valley of 1001 palms' at Vallehermoso

15 AGULO • EMBALSE DE LA PALMITA •
LA PALMITA • LOS ACEVIÑOS • HERMIGUA

Distance: 12.5km/7.8mi; 6h50min   **Map begins on pages 98-99**

Grade: strenuous, with overall ascents/descents of 700m/2300ft on steep and difficult paths (**danger of vertigo**). Many paths are overgrown. Possibility of mists and gale-force winds on the summit. *Only recommended for very experienced walkers with a head for heights.*

Equipment: stout shoes or walking boots, sunhat (tied on!), anorak, cardigan, long trousers, raingear, picnic, water

How to get there: 🚌 to Agulo (Timetable 20)
To return: 🚌 from Hermigua (Timetable 20)

Shorter walk: Agulo — La Palmita — Agulo (8.5km/5.3mi; 4h40min; grade/access as main walk). Follow the main walk to the 2h20min-point, then continue straight up the track. When it ends, cross the small ravine and keep right at a fork. Bear left at the next fork. At a junction turn right and climb to the square in La Palmita. Return the same way for the bus from Agulo (Timetable 20).

Alternative walk: Agulo — El Cedro — Hermigua (19.5km/12mi; 9h20min; grade and access/return as main walk). See notes page 105.

The essence of this walk is a dramatic ascent and an equally dramatic descent. Agulo, your starting point, is the most charming and superbly-sited village on La Gomera. It sits high above the sea in a basin of banana groves, with a magnificent backdrop of towering rock walls. A cliff-hanging path takes you up these very walls. Over the crest lies the farming settlement of La Palmita, a drawn-out sprinkling of houses along the *barranco*. But you climb even higher, onto the escarpment that rises abruptly above Hermigua, in the neighbouring valley. Ravines fall away on either side of you,

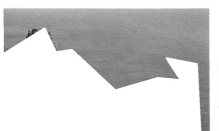

Picnic 15 overlooks Agulo, the most superbly-sited village on the island. The path as far as the picnic spot (lower down the escarpment) is generally wide. Further along in Walk 15, however, it sometimes narrows and can be very vertiginous, as you can see in the lower part of the photograph. You may also be startled by peregrine hawks swooping in and out of the crags nearby, screeching as they dive!

El Cedro — this cottage and its terraced crops are on the route of Alternative walk 15 and can be seen from Walk 16 as well.

revealing stupendous views. Beyond the isolated out-post of Los Aceviños, your descent begins — down razor-sharp ridges, along high and narrow ledges, and finally through vineyards fortified by thick rock walls.

Start out at the bus stop in Agulo: head along the road towards Vallehermoso. Two minutes along, climb stone steps on your right (just beyond a house/shop). At the first junction bear right, then left, and keep straight up to the road. Cross the road and pick up your continuation opposite (a finger-post indicates 'La Palmita'). When you leave the terracing, you begin zigzagging up the rock face (Picnic 15). The bird's-eye view over Agulo — a view you'll long remember — keeps drawing you to a halt. Just before crossing over the pass, you strike a difficult stretch of path — a ledge that literally 'hangs' off the cliff face. Fortunately its width prevents it from being *too* hair-raising. At the top of the pass, the first thing to hit you is the gale-force wind.

A reservoir, the Embalse de la Palmita, seals off the valley up ahead. Keep to the right of a trickling stream and make your way up towards the reservoir. Beyond it, you come down onto a rough, washed-out track. A few minutes up the track pass a fork off to the left and come to a junction: keep left, on the main track. La Palmita comes out of hiding, the houses shuttered, the terraces overgrown. Descending to the floor of the *barranco*, you head deeper into this scattered hamlet. Just as you approach a second bridge (**2h20min**), take the path to the left, heading up a small ridge. *(The Shorter walk crosses the bridge to make for La Palmita.)*

Straight into the ascent pass a house, and three minutes up come to a fork, below another house: keep left*. At the next fork, head right. You leave the heather zone and emerge on the crest. If it's windy, you'll almost be blown back down the ridge! Here the track and eroded hillsides are saturated in volcanic hues,

---

*If this path is overgrown, keep *right* — straight up the ridge. Pass a dwelling and then free-wheel. Keep more or less straight up, through scrub, until you reach the track on the top of the crest; bear right.

from deep mauves to pale orange. You look out over La Palmita. The ridge narrows to a mere blade's width: a corner of Hermigua comes into sight, and then a couple of cottages betray Los Aceviños. Join a road on a curve and follow it to the left. Los Aceviños reappears, a few cottages lost to the outside world. Pass a fork off right to a house, then turn left on a track (**4h20min**). *(The Alternative walk continues to El Cedro; see notes opposite.)*

Referring to the map on these pages, follow the track down into a narrow valley, past a citrus grove. A track joins from the right; ignore it. When your track forks (some 25 minutes along), bear left; then, 50m/yds further on, turn left again, down a wide path. The descent to Hermigua has begun. In wet weather this path is a mud slide. You head down the neck of a ridge, rejoin the track and continue down it to the left. Rounding a ridge, you look straight down the valley as it opens out to the sea. The track narrows into an overgrown path; often you're pushing through scrub. Soon come on to an old cobbled path. Pass a derelict farm building magnificently perched overlooking the valley. Continue straight on past any faint forks, coming into terraced plots shelved high in the valley walls. (These plots may have to be crossed, if the path above them is too overgrown.)

Rounding the lofty wall of a side-ravine, you enter the Barranco de Monteforte (Hermigua's ravine). The valley stretches across in front of you. The route now sidles along the ledge on your right*. When you reach trellised vineyards, your way forks: keep left, down the cobbled path. An *exceedingly steep* descent follows. Take your time, especially if it's wet! Still high in the valley floor, you pass between the first of the houses.

*Should this right turn become hopelessly overgrown, keep *left* beyond this terracing. Scramble down the rocky outcrop below and pick up a faint path built into its left face. Crawl down it and swing left to pass through another overgrown vineyard/garden. Just below it, bear right on a good path, down to the houses. Cross the road once and, on meeting another road, turn left downhill. A minute down descend steps on the left, to the main road. The bus stop is 10 minutes to the left, in front of the church.

Colour and greenery trail down beside you. Cross a road and pick up your continuation some metres/yards uphill on the right. Wide steps take you down through cultivated plots, and you come into the banana belt. Meet the main road: the bus stop is two minutes to the left, by the Agulo/Vallehermoso road sign (**6h50min**).

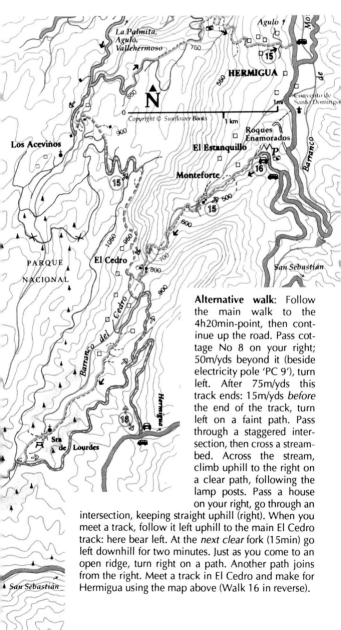

Alternative walk: Follow the main walk to the 4h20min-point, then continue up the road. Pass cottage No 8 on your right; 50m/yds beyond it (beside electricity pole 'PC 9'), turn left. After 75m/yds this track ends: 15m/yds *before* the end of the track, turn left on a faint path. Pass through a staggered intersection, then cross a streambed. Across the stream, climb uphill to the right on a clear path, following the lamp posts. Pass a house on your right, go through an intersection, keeping straight uphill (right). When you meet a track, follow it left uphill to the main El Cedro track: here bear left. At the *next clear* fork (15min) go left downhill for two minutes. Just as you come to an open ridge, turn right on a path. Another path joins from the right. Meet a track in El Cedro and make for Hermigua using the map above (Walk 16 in reverse).

16 MONTEFORTE (HERMIGUA) • EL CEDRO • GARAJONAY • LAS TAJORAS

See map on pages 104-105   **Distance:** 12.5km/7.8mi; 8h

Grade: very strenuous; overall ascent of 1350m/4425ft. **Possibility of vertigo.** Weather is very unpredictable; be prepared for the worst!

Equipment: stout shoes or walking boots, sunhat, cardigan, anorak, gloves, long trousers, raingear, picnic, water

How to get there: Vallehermoso 🚌 (Timetable 20). Ask to be put off at the 'pista de tierra a Monteforte' (the earthen track to Monteforte). *To return:* 🚌 from Las Tajoras (Timetable 19)

Shorter walks

1   Garajonay — El Cedro — Monteforte (8.5km/5.3mi; 3h45min; moderate descent of 1200m/3950ft). 🚗 car or taxi to the Garajonay forestry track (about 2.5km south of Laguna Grande). Or 🚌 to the Chipude/Laguna Grande junction (Timetable 19) and walk the 1.2km to the forestry track. Use the map to walk northeast to Monteforte (the main walk in reverse). The descent is steep in places, and there is a **possibility of vertigo.** Return by bus from Monteforte (Timetable 20).

2   El Cedro turn-off — El Cedro — Nuestra Señora de Lourdes — El Cedro turn-off (10km/6.2mi; 3h; moderate overall descents/ascents of 350m/1150ft). 🚗 or 🚌 (Timetable 19) to/from the El Cedro turn-off. Follow the track to El Cedro (keep right at the junction 25min downhill). In the village, turn left and left again. Then follow the main walk from the 3h25min-point to reach the chapel. Beyond the *ermita*, turn left on a track and, further along, bear right on your outgoing track.

G arajonay, the island's highest summit (1487m/4880ft) spends much of the year veiled in cloud and mist. This accounts for La Gomera's abundant water supply and provides the ideal environment for the *laurisilva* forest. But most of your time will be spent in the Barranco del Cedro — a must for every visitor. A watercourse leads you into its depths, where sheer-sided walls, lavishly draped in vegetation, tower above you. Scaling these walls, you criss-cross an ebullient stream. Reaching the dome of the island, you stumble upon a sprinkling of cottages — El Cedro, set on the edge of the laurel forest. From here nature trails lead you through a dark, damp wood where trees are weighted down with moss, and ferns abound.

Be ready to leave the bus as soon as it passes the turn-off to the reservoir above Hermigua. You want the first track forking off left, just beyond the reservoir. (Coming from Vallehermoso, it's the first turn-off to the right, a couple of minutes above Hermigua.) Just where you alight, you have a fine view over Hermigua and the 'river' of banana groves flooding the ravine floor.

Start out along the track. From a parking area you overlook a rocky salient growing straight up out of the *barranco* wall — this is one of the Roques Enamorados

Near ICONA's picnic site in Garajonay National Park

(Rocks in Love; photograph overleaf). The El Cedro ravine cuts back into the hills on your left, bits and pieces of villages appearing on its terraced walls. Follow the track to the end and descend from it on a path (Picnic 16a). You join a *canal* (watercourse) and remain with it all along the valley. (In places the path is quite difficult and might prove unnerving for inexperienced walkers.) After five minutes or so, you'll have to cross a streambed and rejoin the watercourse; later, go straight over a cobbled path. The ravine slowly closes in on you. Continue up the valley floor and pass a water tank, then swing up behind it on stone-paved steps. A dash of paint is your waymark; more waymarks follow. In a few minutes, the way forks: keep straight on (the right-hand fork); a stone-paved path takes you up the ravine. A series of stream crossings follows, beside rock pools. The way narrows to no more than a passage, and you can see the end — a half-moon cliff-face with a fine veil of water trickling over it. Steps take you up and around a dam wall. From here descend the track into the *barranco* floor, cross the stream, and continue on a path that ascends the right-hand wall of the *barranco*, zigzagging up to the pass.

Close on **3h15min** you're over the pass and looking into El Cedro, a handful of houses set in a cultivated basin, embraced by the laurel forest. Head across plots, keeping left at the forks. Cross the stream and circle behind an enclosed property (*beware:* unchained, unfriendly dog, and equally unfriendly owner). Come onto a track above the property, to find more of this pristine hamlet opening up, ensconced in the hillside folds.

Heading on from El Cedro, keep right at the first junction (met in under a minute) and left at the second (just beyond the first; **3h25min**). Some 6-7 minutes uphill, turn left up a wide path (the first you come to). Several paths strike off left and right, but you remain on an almost level contour, passing straight through an intersection. Reach the 'Caserío del Cedro' sign and enter the forest (and the national park). A wide path leads you up to a small rustic chapel, Nuestra Señora de Lourdes. Past the picnic area and chapel, the small wooden bridge shown on page 107 takes you over the stream and deeper into the forest. Keep left at the fork a few minutes later. This nature trail is maintained by ICONA. You cross another bridge and come onto a forestry track. Some 50m/yds along, rejoin the path, on your right (signposted 'Las Mimbreras'). Pass a path off left and soon cross an overgrown small glade; here you meet an an important junction: veer off right to ascend towards Garajonay. (Soon you will see a sign 'Al Alto de Contadero y de Garajonay'.) You're sometimes tackling healthy undergrowth. Come out onto a flat area and shortly spot a 'Sendero Forestal' (forestry path) sign. Then meet the Laguna Grande road. Cross it and head up the forestry track opposite (signposted for El Contadero/Laguna Grande). Keep left all the way. Weather permitting, you will enjoy a splendid view from the summit of Garajonay (**7h15min**; Picnic 16b), over the undulating hills of the plateau and onto the bold rock shown on the cover, La Fortaleza.

Now go back downhill and take the first left fork (signposted 'Llanos de Crispín/Laguna Grande'). A minute along, bear right. A steep descent follows, along a firebreak collared with heather (ignore a track off to the left). On coming to a staggered junction, keep left. Go left again at the next junction, and ignore the track joining from the right several minutes later. Cut over the crest and descend to a forestry house and your bus stop, on the road below (Las Tajoras; **8h**).

Los Roques Enamorados, from the Barranco del Cedro (Picnic 16a, Walk 16 and Alternative walk 15)

17 HERMIGUA • ENCHEREDA • JARAGAN • SAN SEBASTIAN

Map begins on page 99, continues on page 112, ends on page 67
Distance: 22.5km/14mi; 8h15min
Grade: strenuous, with overall ascents of 750m/2450ft and descents of 850m/2800ft
Equipment: stout shoes or walking boots, sunhat, cardigan, anorak, long trousers, raingear, picnic, plenty of water
How to get there: 🚌 to Hermigua (Timetable 20); get off at the Cepsa petrol station just beyond the church.
To return: 🚌 from San Sebastián (Timetables 19-21)
Shorter walks
1 Hermigua — Playa de la Caleta — El Palmar — Hermigua (10.5km/6.5mi; 4h30min; moderate, with overall ascents of 550m/1800ft and descents of 450m/1475ft; equipment as main walk, plus swimwear). 🚗 or 🚌 (Timetable 20) to/from Hermigua. Follow the main walk to the 45min-point (an ascent), then fork left on a track down to Playa de la Caleta (swimming is safe here when the sea is calm). Head back up the track, then turn off left for El Palmar: your *faint* path is some 50m/yds beyond a water tank that you can see below. Descend into a ravine, cross the streambed, and then take the path climbing into some terraced plots. Some metres/yards up, bear left on another path (you'll spot a red circle waymarker not far along). As the path rounds the hillside (**possibility of vertigo**), keep right at a fork. You cross a streambed full of palms. Beyond here the path is very overgrown, so keep an eye out for the remains of the cobbled path gradually ascending/rounding the hillside. On coming to a house and track, climb the track but, almost immediately (just past a stone building), turn right uphill on a path. It takes you to the main Hermigua track, where you turn right, eventually reaching the pass where you set off down to La Caleta. (For the curious: the sheer-sided valley of Taguluche can be visited from El Palmar; see map page 112.)
2 Camino Forestal de Majona — Jaragán — San Sebastián (11km/6.8mi; 3h35min; easy-moderate ascent of 200m/650ft, followed by a descent of 600m/1970ft; equipment as main walk). Hermigua 🚌 (Timetable 20) to 'Camino Forestal de Majona'. Follow the track up to the pass/parking area; then pick up the main walk at the 5h40min-point. 🚌 from San Sebastián to return (Timetables 19-21)
3 Camino Forestal de Majona — Enchereda — Hermigua (15.5km/9.6mi; 5h; easy-moderate overall ascents of 400m/1300ft and descents of 650m/2150ft; equipment as main walk). Access as Shorter walk 2 above; return by 🚌 from Hermigua (Timetable 20). Follow the track up to the pass/parking area, then use the map on page 112 to continue by track to Enchereda and then Hermigua.

Leaving the lush green banana plantations behind, you ascend the severe walls of the Monteforte Valley and bid farewell to Hermigua. Ahead of you lies one of the loneliest, bleakest corners on the island. This inhospitable landscape of razor-back ridges and sheer ravines may not appeal to everyone. But for those of you who find beauty in desolate landscapes, there are heather-capped crests and a rainbow of volcanic hues in the rock to brighten the way.

Setting out from the petrol station (map page 99), head up the road towards San Sebastián for about 25m/yds. Then descend the first flight of steps that drops into the banana groves. Follow the path across the *barranco* floor. Cross a stream and then keep right when you come onto a wide path. At the end of the path climb up left to the road and turn right. A few minutes along, fork left on a track heading up a gulley (refer now to the map on page 112). Enjoy a view of the ravine's banana plots and Hermigua's beach.

At **45min** you cross the ridge, keeping right. *(Shorter walk 17-1 bears left here.)* An impenetrable wall of mountains crosses the landscape in front of you and tumbles off into the sea. Ascending gradually into the hills, you find them surprisingly green and grassy. Trees begin appearing: short bushy pines, palms and soon junipers. The track maintains an even contour, curling in and out of the hillsides. Ignore all turn-offs until, at about **1h30min**, you leave the track: your turn-off *(easily missed)* is immediately over a culvert crossing a rocky streambed; take the track branching off right, going through an unchained barrier. (At this point, you can see an oblong, dilapidated farm building draped in grape vines below on the El Palmar track, just a few minutes away.) Now a tortuous, steep climb lies ahead.

Not far off the main road, on the Camino Forestal de Majona (main walk and Shorter walks 16-2 and 16-3). Los Roques are seen in the distance. On La Gomera you pass through a countryside where time stands still and nature has the upper hand. Captivating landscapes unravel as you huff and puff your way across the mountainous terrain, winding in and out of plunging ravines. A cobweb of old village paths stretches across the entire island, and picture-book scenes greet you from every crest. But you need not be a walker to appreciate all the beauty: from Car tours 5 and 6, for example, you'll enjoy views quite similar to this (see photograph page 31).

Soon you pass through vineyards and come into a colony of palms. Rock walls dripping with vegetation rise sharply above you. As you approach the crest, the banana plantations of Hermigua come into view again. Eventually you're below a couple of stone farm sheds and an orchard set high on the escarpment. What a tremendous vista this settlement commands across tumbling naked ridges and out over the rocky shoreline onto a white-capped sea. Further on, off a sharp bend, you look down into a plunging ravine full of vineyards; the vertical walls of this *barranco* are speckled with bright green houseleeks. Reaching the tree-line, you come into pine forest with a touch of laurel in its midst. A wooden barrier is met at **3h30min**, when you cross over the *cumbre* and get blasted by the wind.

Continuing deeper into this wilderness, you drop down into a quiet, out-of-the-way valley. Cloaks of heather slip down off the shoulders of the crests. Flocks graze the lower grassy slopes, and you'll bump into healthy cows and calves dawdling along the track. Please, pass them quietly. Later, when you enter another valley, neglected plots and the remains of stone walls tell the story of homesteads abandoned. It's quiet here, the only sounds you'll hear are the shrills of the kestrel and the fleeing quail. A makeshift gate closes off

the track some minutes along. Again, please leave it as you find it. Heading into yet another valley, the lone homestead of Enchereda comes into sight, blending in with the browns of the surrounding denuded hills. Its entourage of palm trees gives it away. Reach this rustic outpost at **5h**. The goats are milked at midday. You can

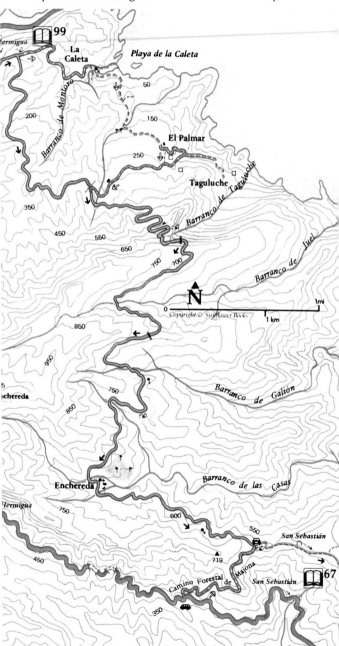

buy *queso ahumado* (smoked cheese) here; the best cheese on the island comes from these hills and valleys. Along here the eroded hillsides are a feast of colour: maroon, russet, faded gold, rusty orange. Heading out of the valley, your way is no more than a ledge cut along the sheer side of a ridge. Some 25 minutes from Enchereda, a water tap below the track allows you to top up your canteens. Soon you catch sight of bright orange lichen smeared across the maroon hillsides.

On reaching a pass (**5h40min**), look down over the Barranco de Aguajilva, one of the valleys leading to San Sebastián. The main north road is below. *(From here Shorter walk 17-2 joins the main walk and 17-3 heads north to Hermigua.)* Leave the track: take the path heading east, off the parking area. Twin stripes of paint (orange and white) mark the entrance to the path and keep you on the route across the rocky hillside. Soon you're standing in front of a craggy outcrop looking up into a cave. The path sidles up against the sheer face of the ridge, which slides down into the *barranco.* Minutes further along (**6h**; see map page 67), a path climbs left to Jaragán, a solitary homestead high in the rock above.

Continue straight on here, beside white- and pink-hued rock. You reach another crest, from where it is a little difficult to locate your continuing route: barely a minute along the crest, you'll see a path cutting in front of you. (Keep an eye out for small cairns and the orange and white paint.) Veer left along this path and come to a rock with orange and white paint splashes some 100m/yds along. Here turn off and head downhill to the right on an *invisible* path; small cairns and the paint are your only guides for the first few minutes. When you are sure of your route, stop and admire the views! You descend a winding (potentially ankle-twisting) path into a side-ravine. When a path joins from the left some 15-20 minutes down, keep straight on (the right-hand fork). Cross a dyke and later enter the Barranco del Rincón, a narrow, dry ravine lined with crumbled stone walls from top to bottom. A faint path joins from the left, and you soon pass a television aerial cemented into the ridge. Pass through a stone wall of terracing and keep straight down the top of the crest. Join a track which brings you onto another track: keep right and head down to the outskirts of San Sebastián. Follow the road straight down and then turn right to the *mirador,* from where steps descend to the centre (**8h15min**).

Appendix

Information of particular interest to walkers is found on the following nine pages. We have included as much information about the whole of Tenerife as possible in this book, but do remember that to explore the whole island *on foot*, you will need the companion volume, *Landscapes of Tenerife (Teno • Orotava • Anaga • Cañadas).*

BUS AND FERRY TIMETABLES

Below is a list of destinations on Tenerife (T) and La Gomera (G) covered by the following timetables. Numbers following places names are **timetable** numbers. There are more buses *and departures* than those listed here; see latest TITSA timetables.

Adeje (T) 7, 10
Aguamansa (T) 11
Agulo (G) 20
Alajeró (G) 21
Arafo (T) 8
Arona (T) 4
Arure (G) 19
Bailadero, El (T) 14
Bajamar (T) 13
Buenavista (T) 12
Caldera, La (T) 11
Cañadas, Las (T) 4
Candelaria, La (T) 3, 8, 9

Carboneras, Las (T) 16
Cedro, El (G) 19
Chipude (G) 19
Cristianos, Los (T) 2-4, 7, 10; *see also ferries, page* 119
Degollada de Peraza (G) 21
Erque junction (G) 19
Gigantes, Los (T) 10
Granadilla (T) 5-7, 9

Guía de Isora (T) 7
Güímar (T) 6, 8
Hayas, Las (G) 19
Hermigua (G) 20
Icod de los Vinos (T) 12
Igueste (T) 15
Laguna, La (T) 1, 13, 16-18
Orotava, La (T) 11
Parador (T) 4
Pico del Inglés (T) 16-18
Playa de las Amé-

ricas (T) 2-4, 7, 10
Portillo, El (T) 4
Puerto de la Cruz (T) 1, 2, 11, 12
Punta del Hidalgo (T) 13
Río de Arico, El (T) 6, 9
Rosas, Las (G) 20
San Andrés (T) 14, 15
San Juán, Playa de (T) 10

San Sebastián (G) 19-21; *see also ferries, page* 119
Santa Cruz (T) 1, 3, 6, 8, 9, 13-15
Santiago, Playa de (G) 21
Taganana (T) 14
Tajoras, Las (G) 19
Valle Gran Rey (G) 19
Vallehermoso (G) 20
Vilaflor (T) 4, 5

BUS SERVICES — TENERIFE

1 🚌 102: Santa Cruz to Puerto de la Cruz; EXPRESS; daily

Santa Cruz	La Laguna	Puerto
07.30	07.45	08.30
	then every 30 minutes until	
20.30	20.45	21.30
21.15	21.30	22.15
Puerto	**La Laguna**	**Santa Cruz**
07.17	08.00	08.15
	then every 30 minutes until	
21.15	22.00	22.15

2 🚌 343: Playa de las Américas to Puerto de la Cruz; EXPRESS; daily

Playa Américas	Los Cristianos	El Botánico	Puerto
09.00	09.10	10.50	11.00
11.30	11.40	13.20	13.30
15.30	15.40	17.20	17.30
17.45	17.55	19.35	19.45
Puerto	**El Botánico**	**Los Cristianos**	**Playa Américas**
09.00	09.10	10.50	11.00
11.10	11.20	13.00	13.10
15.20	15.40	17.10	17.20
17.40	17.50	19.30	19.40

3 🚌 111: Santa Cruz to Playa de las Américas; daily

Santa Cruz	La Candelaria	Poris de Abona	Los Cristianos	Playa Américas
		Mondays to Fridays		
06.00	06.15	06.50	07.25	07.30
		and every 40minutes until		
20.40	20.55	21.30	22.05	22.10
		Saturdays, Sundays and holidays		
06.30	06.45	07.20	07.55	08.00
		and every hour on the half hour until		
21.30	21.45	22.20	22.55	23.0
Playa Américas	**Los Cristianos**	**Poris de Abona**	**La Candelaria**	**Santa Cruz**
		Mondays to Fridays		
06.00	06.05	06.40	07.15	07.30
		and every 40minutes until		
21.20	21.25	22.00	22.35	22.50
		Saturdays, Sundays and holidays		
06.30	06.35	07.10	07.45	08.00
		and every hour on the half hour until		
21.30	21.35	22.10	22.45	23.00

4 🚌 342: Playa de las Américas to Las Cañadas; daily

Playa de las Américas (depart)	09.15	**El Portillo** (depart)	15.15
Los Cristianos	09.30	**Montaña Blanca**	15.30
Arona	09.40	**Teide funicular**	15.40
Vilaflor	10.00	**Parador**	16.00
Parador	11.00	**Vilaflor**	17.00
Teide funicular	11.15	**Arona**	17.20
Montaña Blanca	11.30	**Los Cristianos**	17.30
El Portillo	11.45	**Playa de las Américas**	17.45

5 🚌 474: Granadilla to Vilaflor; *Mondays to Fridays only*

Granadilla	Vilaflor		Vilaflor	Granadilla
09.15	10.15		10.15	11.15
14.15	15.15		15.15	16.15
18.15	19.15		19.15	20.15

6 🚌 125: Santa Cruz to Granadilla; daily

Santa Cruz	Güimar	El Río de Arico	Granadilla
05.00	06.00	07.00	07.15
09.30	10.30	11.30	11.45
14.15	15.15	16.15	16.30
17.30	18.30	19.30	19.45
Granadilla	**El Río de Arico**	**Güimar**	**Santa Cruz**
05.30	05.45	06.45	07.45
09.15	09.30	10.30	11.30
13.30	13.45	14.45	15.45
18.30	18.45	19.45	20.45

7 🚌 416: Granadilla to Guía de Isora; daily

Granadilla	Playa Américas	Adeje	Guía de Isora
05.30	06.00	06.15	06.45
	and every hour on the half hour until		
20.30	21.00	21.15	21.45
Guía de Isora	**Adeje**	**Playa Américas**	**Granadilla**
08.30	09.00	09.15	09.45
	and every hour on the half hour until		
20.30	21.00	21.15	21.45

8 🚌 121: Santa Cruz to Güimar; daily

Santa Cruz	La Candelaria	Arafo	Güimar
		Mondays to Fridays	
06.15	06.30	07.05	07.15
	and every hour at 15 minutes past the hour until		
20.15	20.30	21.05	21.15
		Saturdays, Sundays and holidays	
07.45	08.00	08.35	08.45
	and every 2 hours at 45 minutes past the hour until		
19.45	20.00	20.35	20.45
Güimar	**Arafo**	**La Candelária**	**Santa Cruz**
		Mondays to Fridays	
05.45	05.55	06.30	06.45
	and every hour at 45 minutes past the hour until		
19.45	19.55	20.30	20.45
		Saturdays, Sundays and holidays	
05.45	05.55	06.30	06.45
	and every 2 hours at 45 minutes past the hour until		
19.45	19.55	20.30	20.45

9 🚌 116: Santa Cruz to Granadilla; daily*

Santa Cruz	La Candelaria	Lombo de Arico	El Río de Arico	Granadilla
06.00	06.15	07.00	07.20	07.45
		and every 2 hours until		
18.00	18.15	19.00	19.20	19.45
Granadilla	**El Río de Arico**	**Lombo de Arico**	**La Candelaria**	**Santa Cruz**
07.30	07.55	08.15	09.00	09.15
10.00	10.25	10.45	11.30	11.45
		and then every 2 hours until		
20.00	20.25	20.45	21.30	21.45

*via the motorway and stopping only at the motorway exit for these villages

10 🚐 473: Las Galletas to Los Gigantes; daily*

Las Galletas	Playa Américas	Adeje	Playa San Juán	Los Gigantes
07.30	07.45	08.00	08.25	08.40
		and every hour on the half hour until		
20.30	20.45	21.00	21.25	21.40
Los Gigantes	**Playa San Juán**	**Adeje**	**Playa Américas**	**Las Galletas**
06.30	06.45	07.10	07.25	07.40
		and every hour on the half hour until		
21.30	31.45	22.10	22.25	22.40

*all departure times are *approximate* except departures from Las Galletas and Los Gigantes

11 🚌 345: Puerto de la Cruz to La Caldera; daily

Puerto	La Orotava	Aguamansa	La Caldera
08.00*	08.15*	09.00*	—
08.45	09.00	09.45	09.50
	and every 45 minutes until		
17.15	17.30	18.15	18.20
La Caldera	**Aguamansa**	**La Orotava**	**Puerto**
10.00	10.05	10.50	11.05
	and every 45 minutes until		
18.25	18.30	19.15	19.30
—	19.15*	20.00*	20.15*
—	20.00*	20.45*	21.00*
—	20.45**	21.30**	—
—	21.15*	22.00*	22.15*

*terminates/starts out from Aguamansa; **only to La Orotava

12 🚌 363: Puerto de la Cruz to Buenavista; daily

Puerto	San Juán	Icod de los Vinos	Buenavista
06.00	06.20	06.45	07.45
	and every hour on the hour until		
22.00	22.20	22.45	23.45

Buenavista	Icod de los Vinos	San Juán	Puerto
06.30	07.30	07.55	08.15
	and every hour on the hour until		
20.30*	21.30*	—	—

*the bus at 20.30 terminates at Icod de los Vinos; all others go through to Puerto

13 🚌 105: Santa Cruz to Punta del Hidalgo; daily

Santa Cruz	La Laguna	Tegueste	Bajamar	Punta Hidalgo
07.35	08.05	08.20	08.30	08.45
		and every 30min until		
19.35	20.05	20.20	20.30	20.45

Punta Hidalgo	Bajamar	Tegueste	La Laguna	Santa Cruz
08.00	08.10	08.25	08.40	09.10
		and every 30min until		
20.00	20.10	20.25	20.40	21.10

14 🚌 246: Santa Cruz to Almáciga; daily

Santa Cruz	San Andrés	El Bailadero	Taganana	Almáciga
		Mondays to Fridays		
06.50	07.00	07.25	07.35	07.40
10.30	10.40	11.05	11.15	11.20
13.10	13.20	13.45	13.55	14.00
		Saturdays, Sundays and holidays		
07.05	07.15	07.40	07.50	07.55
09.10	09.20	09.45	09.55	10.00
11.30	11.40	12.05	12.15	12.20
14.10	14.20	14.45	14.55	15.00

Almáciga	Taganana	El Bailadero	San Andrés	Santa Cruz
		Mondays to Fridays		
14.10*	14.20*	14.30*	14.55*	—
15.45	15.55	16.05	16.30	16.40
18.00	18.10	18.20	18.45	18.55
20.05	20.15	20.25	20.50	21.00
		Saturdays, Sundays and holidays		
12.45	12.55	13.05	13.30	13.40
15.15	15.25	15.35	16.00	16.10
17.45	17.55	18.05	18.30	18.40
20.15	20.25	14.35	21.00	21.10

*only to San Andrés

15 🚌 245: Santa Cruz to Igueste; daily

Santa Cruz	Igueste	Mondays to Fridays	Igueste	Santa Cruz
07.25	07.55		12.30	13.00
09.10	09.40		15.10	15.40
11.50	12.20		17.10	17.40
14.25	14.55		19.10	19.40
16.10	16.40		21.10	21.40
08.40	09.10	Sat, Sun/holidays	13.30	14.00
10.30	11.00		15.30	16.00
12.30	13.00		19.30	20.00
14.30	15.00		21.30	22.00

Departures from San Andrés about 15min after Santa Cruz (outbound) or Igueste (inbound)

16 🚌 1.705: La Laguna to Las Carboneras and Taborno; daily**

		Winter: Mondays to Fridays		
La Laguna	Cruz del Carmen	Casa Negrín	Las Carboneras	Taborno
09.15	09.35	09.40	09.55	10.10
15.15	15.35	15.40	15.55	16.10
Taborno	Las Carboneras	Casa Negrín	Cruz del Carmen	La Laguna
16.30	16.15	16.45	16.50	17.10
19.30	19.15	19.45	19.50	20.10

Summer: Mondays to Fridays and year-round: Saturdays, Sundays and holidays

La Laguna	Cruz del Carmen	Casa Negrín	Las Carboneras	Taborno
07.30	07.50	07.55	08.10	08.25
15.00	15.20	15.25	15.40	15.55
Taborno	Las Carboneras	Casa Negrín	Cruz del Carmen	La Laguna
16.00	15.45	16.30	16.35	16.55
19.30*	19.15*	19.45*	19.50*	20.10*

*Not on Saturdays, Sundays or holidays

17 🚌 1.706: La Laguna to Afur and Roque Negro; daily**

		Winter: Mondays to Fridays		
La Laguna	Casa Negrín	Casa Forestal	Roque Negro	Afur
13.15	*not known*	14.05	14.20	14.30
Afur	Roque Negro	Casa Forestal*	Casa Negrín**	La Laguna
14.45	14.55	15.10	*not known*	16.00
17.45	17.55	18.10	*not known*	19.00
20.00	20.10	20.25	*not known*	21.15

Summer: Mondays to Fridays

La Laguna	Casa Negrín	Casa Forestal	Roque Negro	Afur
06.55	*not known*	07.45	08.00	08.10
13.15	*not known*	14.05	14.20	14.30
Afur	Roque Negro	Casa Forestal*	Casa Negrín**	La Laguna
14.45	14.55	15.10	*not known*	16.00
17.45	17.55	18.10	*not known*	19.00
19.45	19.55	20.10	*not known*	21.00

Year-round: Saturdays, Sundays and holidays

La Laguna	Casa Negrín	Casa Forestal	Roque Negro	Afur
07.00	*not known*	07.50	08.05	08.15
13.15	*not known*	14.05	14.20	14.30
Afur	Roque Negro	Casa Forestal*	Casa Negrín**	La Laguna
14.45	14.55	15.10	*not known*	16.00
17.45	17.55	18.10	*not known*	19.00

*Also called 'Cruz de Taganana'; **bus should pass Casa Negrín, but *verify in advance!*

18 🚌 1.708: La Laguna to Pico del Inglés; daily**

	Winter: Mondays to Fridays and Sundays and holidays all year		
La Laguna	Pico del Inglés*	Pico del Inglés*	La Laguna
10.15	10.45	10.45	11.15

	Summer: Mondays to Fridays and Saturdays all year		
La Laguna	Pico del Inglés*	Pico del Inglés*	La Laguna
09.15	09.45	09.45	10.15

*turn-off to

**Operated by TRAMSMERSA out of the main bus station (shared with TITSA) by the motorway in La Laguna. From the Playas, take bus 111 to Santa Cruz, then bus 102 to La Laguna. Departure times change frequently: pick up a timetable or telephone in advance: 250740. Should these routes become part of the TITSA network in future, the same bus station will be used.

BUS SERVICES — LA GOMERA

NB: All bus departures **must** be checked **before** planning a walk; times change frequently, or buses do not run due to local holidays. Arrival and departure times can vary by as much as half an hour!

19 🚌: San Sebastián to Valle Gran Rey; *not Sundays*

San Sebastián	El Cedro*	Cruz Zarcita	Alajeró*	Las Tajoras
12.00	12.35	12.40	12.45	12.50
18.00	18.35	18.40	18.45	18.50

Erque*	Chipude**	Las Hayas	Arure	Valle Gran Rey
12.52	12.55	13.20	13.35	14.00
18.52	18.55	19.30	19.35	20.00

Valle Gran Rey	Arure	Las Hayas	Chipude**	Erque*
04.00	04.25	04.40	05.05	05.08
14.30	14.55	15.10	15.35	15.38

Las Tajoras	Alajeró	Cruz Zarita	El Cedro*	San Sebastián
05.10	05.15	05.20	05.25	06.00
15.40	15.45	15.50	15.55	16.30

*turn-off to; **10-minute stop

20 🚌: San Sebastián to Vallehermoso; daily

San Sebastián	Hermigua	Agulo	Las Rosas	Vallehermoso
12.00	12.35	12.50	13.00	13.25
13.00*	13.35*	13.50*	14.00*	14.25*
18.00**	18.35**	18.50**	19.00**	19.25**

Vallehermoso	Las Rosas	Agulo	Hermigua	San Sebastián
06.00	06.25	06.35	06.50	07.25
08.30*	08.55*	09.05*	09.20*	09.55*
15.00**	15.25**	15.35**	15.50**	16.25**

*not Saturdays, Sundays or holidays; **not Sundays or holidays

21 🚌: San Sebastián to Playa de Santiago and Alajeró; *not Sundays*

San Sebastián	Degollada de Peraza	Playa de Santiago	Alajeró*
12.00	12.35	13.15	14.00
18.00	18.35	19.15	20.00

Alajeró*	Playa de Santiago	Degollada de Peraza	San Sebastián
05.15	06.00	06.40	07.15
14.00	14.30	15.10	15.45

*bus to and from Alajeró only runs Mon, Wed, Fri

INTER-ISLAND FERRY/HYDROFOIL SERVICES

To travel from Playa de las Américas/Los Cristianos: The ticket office opens one hour before the sailing times

To travel from Santa Cruz: Arrive at the Santa Cruz bus station at least two hours before the sailing. You can buy your ferry/hydrofoil ticket there before boarding the bus (bus departs 1h45min before sailing time)

'Vila de Agaete' and 'Benchijigua' Ferry Services; daily; journey time 90min
depart Los Cristianos 09.00, 09.30, 14.45, 15.30, 20.00
depart San Sebastián (La Gomera) 07.00, 11.00*, 12.30, 17.15, 18.00

'Barracuda' Hydrofoil Service; daily; journey time 35min
departs Los Cristianos 08.00, 10.00, 15.00, 17.00
departs San Sebastián (La Gomera) 09.00, 11.00, 16.00, 18.00

*13.30 on Sundays

Where to stay

It's more than likely that you are based in the **south of Tenerife**, at Los Cristianos or Playa de las Américas. If you've rented a car, the entire island is within easy reach — see our tours and touring map. A few superb walks are also nearby (Walks 1-5 in this book). Another advantage of staying in the south is the proximity of La Gomera. The ferry departs from Los Cristianos daily at 09.00 and 09.30; the hydrofoil at 08.00 and 10.00; both are ideal for day trips. The bus service in the south is excellent — so good that you might also consider exploring the Anaga via Santa Cruz: use the companion volume, *Landscapes of Tenerife.*

If the sight of concrete jungles 'turns you off', try the more humble villages of El Medano, Adeje, Granadilla, or San Juán — not so well served by transport, with a simpler standard of accommodation, and further afield. Consider spending a night at the Parador de las Cañadas before setting out on Walk 5 — a perfect treat! To book in advance, telephone 922-38 64 15.

On your next visit, *if you really want to see Tenerife on foot,* your best base would be either Puerto or Santa Cruz: see *Landscapes of Tenerife.*

Exploring **La Gomera** from a base in southern Tenerife is the way most visitors will first become acquainted with this little-developed gem of an island. The car tours and some short walks are perfectly feasible.

But to get to know La Gomera on foot, you will want to be staying on the island. No one place is better than another as a base — but the north does have the advantage of a better bus service. Valle Gran Rey is where most visitors stay, followed by Playa de Santiago and San Sebastián. All three offer a reasonable standard of accommodation — generally in apartments and rooms. The only hotels on the island are in Santiago and San Sebastián (the *parador*). But many other villages offer accommodation in pensions and apartments (information available at the car rental office in the main square in San Sebastián). With interest in La Gomera growing, these are often booked up. Moving around can be lots of fun, and of course you'll have a better choice of walks. Remember: always reserve your accommodation by telephone the night before, to avoid disappointment! If you have no desire to move around, you'll have to rely on hire cars and taxis for connecting transport on many of the walks (see pages 45 and 46:

'Transport on La Gomera' and 'Walking times'). Camping outside the National Park is an accepted and common practice amongst young travellers. It is forbidden to camp anywhere inside the National Park. Finally, if you plan to spend considerable time on the island — a month or more — you can often find a house to rent in the smaller out-of-the-way villages. The best way to find these is by enquiring at the local shops and bars.

Walkers' checklist
The following points cannot be stressed too often:

- **At any time a walk may become unsafe** due to storm damage or road works. If the route is not as described in this book, and your way ahead is not secure, do not attempt to go on.
- **Walks for experts only** may be unsuitable for winter, and all mountain walks may be hazardous then
- **Never walk alone**. Four is the best walking group: if someone is injured, two can go for help, and there will be no need for panic in an emergency.
- **Do not overestimate your energies** — your speed will be determined by the slowest walker in your group.
- **Transport connections** at the end of a walk are vital.
- **Proper shoes or boots** are a necessity.
- **Mists** can suddenly appear on the higher elevations.
- **Warm clothing** is needed in the mountains; even in summer take some along, in case you are delayed.
- **Compass, whistle, torch, first-aid kit** weigh little, but might save your life.
- **Extra rations** must be taken on long walks.
- **Always take a sunhat with you**, and in summer a cover-up for your arms and legs as well.
- **A stout stick** is a help on rough terrain and to discourage the rare unfriendly dog.

Lagarto Canarión

Spanish for walkers
In the tourist centres you hardly need know any Spanish at all. But once out in the countryside, a few words of Spanish will be helpful, especially if you lose your way. Here's a way to communicate in Spanish that

is (almost) foolproof. First, memorise the few short key questions and their possible answers given below. Then, when you have your 'mini-speech' memorised, always ask the many questions you can concoct from it **in such a way that you get a 'sí' (yes) or 'no' answer**. Never ask an open-ended question such as 'Where is the main road?' Instead, ask the question and then *suggest the most likely answer yourself*. For instance: 'Good day, sir. Please — where is the path to Erque? *Is it straight ahead?*' Now, unless you get a *'sí'* response, try: *'Is it to the left?'* If you go through the list of answers to your own question, you will eventually get a *'sí'* response — probably with a vigorous nod of the head — and this is more reassuring than relying solely on sign language. Following are the two most likely situations in which you may have to practice some Spanish. The dots (...) show where you will fill in the name of your destination. Approximate pronunciation of place names is given in the Index opposite.

Asking the way
The key questions

English	Spanish	pronounced as
Good day,	Buenos días	**Boo**-eh-nos **dee**-ahs
sir (madam, miss).	señor (señora, señorita).	sen-**yor** (sen-**yor**-ah sen-yor-**ee**-tah).
Please —	Por favor —	**Poor** fah-**voor** —
where is	dónde está	**dohn**-day es-**tah**
the road to ... ?	la carretera a ...?	la cah-reh-**teh**-rah ah ...?
the footpath to ...?	la senda de ...?	lah **sen**-dah day ...?
the way to ...?	el camino a ...?	el cah-**mee**-noh ah ...?
the bus stop?	la parada?	lah par-**rah**-dah?
Many thanks.	Muchas gracias.	**Moo**-chas **gra**-thee-as.

Possible answers

English	Spanish	pronounced as
is it here?	está aquí?	es-**tah** ah-**kee**?
straight ahead?	todo recto?	**toh**-doh **rec**-toh?
behind?	detrás?	day-**tras**?
to the right?	a la derecha?	ah lah day-**reh**-chah?
to the left?	a la izquierda?	ah lah eeth-kee-**er**-dah?
above/below?	arriba/abajo?	ah-**ree**-bah/ah-**bah**-hoh?

Asking a taxi driver to return for you

English	Spanish	pronounced as
Please	Por favor	**Poor** fah-**voor**
take us to ...	llévanos a ...	l-**yay**-vah-nos ah ...
and return	y volver	ee vol-**vair**
for us at ...	para nosotros a ...	**pah**-rah nos-**oh**-tros ah ...

Point out the time when you wish him to return on your watch.

Perenquiez

 Index

Geographical names only are included here; for non-geographical entries, see Contents, page 3. To save space, some entries have been grouped together under the following headings: *Barranco* (riverbed, ravine), *Ermita* (chapel), *Mirador* (viewpoint), *Playa* (beach), *Punta* (point), *Roque* (rock), and *Zona recreativa* (picnic area with tables). A page number in *italic type* indicates a map; a page number in **bold type** a photograph. Either of these may be in addition to a text reference on the same page. 'TT': see Timetable index on page 114. Approximate pronunciation is included. (T) Tenerife; (G) La Gomera.

123

Country code for walkers and motorists

The experienced rambler is used to following a 'country code' on his walks, but the tourist out for a lark may unwittingly cause damage, harm animals, and even endanger his own life. A code for behaviour is important wherever people roam over the countryside, but especially so on Tenerife and La Gomera, where the rugged terrain (and unexpected cold weather) can lead to dangerous mistakes.

- **Only light fires** at picnic areas with fireplaces. Stub out cigarettes with care.
- **Do not frighten animals**. The goats and sheep you may encounter on your walks are not tame. By making loud noises or trying to touch or photograph them, you may cause them to run in fear and be hurt.
- **Walk quietly** through all hamlets and villages and take care not to provoke the dogs. Ignore their barking and keep your walking stick out of sight.
- **Leave all gates just as you found them**, whether they are at farms or on the mountainside. Although you may not see any animals, the gates *do* have a purpose: they keep animals in (or out of) an area. Again, animals could be endangered by careless behaviour.
- **Protect all wild and cultivated plants**. Don't try to pick wild flowers or uproot saplings. They will die before you even get back to your hotel. Obviously fruit and other crops are someone's private property and should not be touched. ***Never walk over cultivated land.***
- **Take all your litter away with you.**
- **DO NOT TAKE RISKS!** This is the most important point of all. Do not attempt walks beyond your capacity, and do not wander off the paths described if there is any sign of mist or if it is late in the day. **Never walk alone**, and *always* tell a responsible person *exactly* where you are going and what time you plan to return. Remember, if you become lost or injure yourself, it may be a long time before you are found. On any but a very short walk near villages, be sure to take a first-aid kit, whistle, torch, compass, extra water and warm clothing — as well as some high-energy food, like chocolate.